A
PLACE
FOR
GRAYSON

Kaitlin Kalagher

ISBN: 978-0-578-58285-6

Book design by Isabel Robalo

Printed in the Unites States of America

Dedication

To my brother, Gregory James.
I miss you. I love you.

Prologue

I don't know if I'm alive.

I'm woken by a bright pink beam of light coming from the window next to my bed. A soft melody plays in my head. One that I can remember hearing from the church organ when I was younger. My limbs feel light as though they are filling up with helium. What is going on?

I must be in some sort of bizarre dream where you can't distinguish what is fake and what is a reality.

I shift my focus down toward my hands placed on my thighs. I rub my palms against my jeans, but I don't feel anything.

I leave my bedroom and head downstairs with caution because something in this house just doesn't feel right—I don't feel right. I don't remember when I fell asleep last night, or what I had for dinner even. Did I get *that* fucked up?

As I round the corner at the bottom of the staircase, I call out to my brother Michael. No answer. Maybe he considered going to the skate park before it got too hot. I search each room, only to find an empty house creeping with silence. Mom isn't here either.

I have a sense of uneasiness like when you watch your first rated R movie when you're not supposed to. You're just waiting for your parents to catch you any second.

I peek up at the calendar, and it still reads Wednesday, August 2nd— I guess Mom hasn't crossed today off yet. I sit at the kitchen table and stare into a stained-glass decoration of purple and turquoise Nana had given Mom—the last precious gift she gave before her son left us for good. I catch my vision starting to blur, but I don't dare to blink. I begin to remember Nana coming to visit when I was little and how she made the best chocolate chip cookies. We would stay up all night watching movies, and she would whisper, "don't tell your mother." I always giggled back and promised her I would never tell Mom that we were up till 2am drinking Coca-Cola all night. I want these memories to last, so I stare a little longer until my eyes are burning and completely filled with water.

I'm overcome by the darkness of the truth, that Nana is gone, and that instead of drinking soda and watching movies, I'm worrying about the next time I'm going to get high. I'm ashamed of who I've become.

I sprint to the bathroom because of the ensuing panic, which is often followed by excessive vomiting. My breathing gradually becomes more rapid and shallow. I am breathing with so much force that I don't feel like I'm breathing at all.

I'm staring at myself in the mirror, but for a second I don't even know if it's me. I'm not looking at Grayson anymore. This person gawks back at me with clammy skin and bloodshot eyes. The wrinkles next to his nose protrude vertically down to his mouth, and he looks as if he hasn't slept in years. His mouth is bone dry and his clothes dirty. The marks on his arm look painful.

He is sad and lost as though he doesn't have a person in the world who loves him anymore—not even himself. An aura of depression hovers over him as he stares blankly back at me.

What happened to him?

Now

Grayson

This building must be at least a hundred years old. It stands right off Route 4 at the beginning of town. The outside frame looks somewhat unbalanced and the landscape is poorly maintained, if at all. The outside paint peels upward, and in some places, the wood is naked of any color. A large rhododendron stands five feet tall in the front of the building. Weeds scatter the premise and even stick out of cracks in the sidewalk. The parking lot in the back has a few potholes that I assume the town does not wish to fill. This place reminds me of one of those horror movies when a new family thinks they are moving into a beautiful, historic home, but end up haunted by the ghosts of people who had once lived there.

I stay in my car for a few minutes, waiting for a few more cars to pull in. Two people are here before me, causing me to wonder if I am in the right place. They appear old, one with grey hair and wrinkles on her neck she cannot hide with a turtleneck. The man, about the same age, is not nearly as old-looking as the woman next to him. He's bald and wears glasses an inch thick. They do not speak to each other.

I know I have the correct address, but maybe the meeting place has changed. Had those two people not been here when I pulled in, I would have assumed this ancient-looking place had been abandoned.

A couple of minutes before 8 am, I step out of my car onto the rigid pavement and walk towards the front door. Cobwebs and rust cover the entrance. The doorknob is rough with dots of rust from the rain, so I turn it with force to see if it's open. The door is unlocked. I invite myself in. It's a large room, probably once a living room.

A chill moves up my spine, and for a moment, I wish I had not come. I look down at my watch, realizing I'm technically two minutes early. I hesitantly walk toward the group of people who have turned their heads in my direction after the door slams shut behind me. I'm not sure if they have started yet. They stay silent as I walk toward them.

"My name is Grayson, and I am an addict," I say to the faces staring at me. We sit in a circle resembling reading time in kindergarten. In those days, we had an area rug in front of the chalkboard that was covered in different colored shapes—squares of blue and trapezoids of red. We'd align ourselves in a circle by each sitting on a colored shape of our choice. That's basically what we look like here except we aren't a bunch of five-year-olds and we're sitting in chairs, not on shapes.

After speaking aloud, my heart continues to race, and I'm convinced the person next to me can hear each beat. Nervous that I have just given my identity away to strangers, I freeze with every cell in my body, going numb. The annoyance that evolves from the lump in my throat forces me to gulp louder than normal. I look around quietly and question whether I should say something else. I don't talk anymore, though. I decide that I've already said enough. I stay quiet in my seat and wait for someone else to start talking. As the seconds of my silence pass, my heart slows, and my anxiety subsides.

I am like a tourist here, not knowing a sense of direction in unfamiliar territory. I'm uncomfortable knowing that I don't understand how these meetings necessarily work. It's as if I'm on vacation without an itinerary, and no one is around for guidance.

The large room crawls with hollow echoes as footsteps slowly approach the circle. I level out my head and watch as a girl with light green eyes and curly brown hair enters the loop of people. She walks straight toward me and sits down on my left, ignoring the three other chairs that have no one sitting in them.

The curly-haired girl peeks over at me as if very curious to see if I've noticed. *Of course, I have*, I think to myself. She's beautiful. Her eyelashes are super long, and her skin is immaculate, absent of blemishes and freckles. She is thin and appears to be in shape. Perhaps she's runner. As I embrace her features, she looks over to me and catches me staring. I detect a burning rage of blood migrate from the core of my body up into the apples of my cheeks. I can see her in my peripheral, nonchalantly focusing on me. I don't look at her again.

I keep my head tilted downward, staring at my sweaty hands that I have clasped together in between my knees. The entire time I am here, I feel like the world is staring at me even though there are no more than ten people in this room.

As I look around, I determine that no one here is like me. Most everyone here seems to be thirty-five years old or older. Except her.

She starts talking, and I can tell by her relaxed tone that this isn't her first time here. She explains to the group that her name is Emily and goes into detail about her battle with alcohol.

There's a specific story she tells that shocks me because she is so beautiful and innocent looking. One night after she got in a fight with her now ex-boyfriend, she got so belligerently drunk that she broke into his house and smashed his flat screen tv after flipping all the living room furniture over. Her ex called the police and had her arrested.

At this point in the story, her voice becomes dry and starts to crack. Her parents were so disappointed with how she had been acting that they left her in jail. They told her she wasn't welcome at home with her drinking habits. She stops talking and I hope to myself that they let her back in with them.

How could someone banish their child like that? She needed help. How was she supposed to know this demon would overcome her so quickly that there would be no time to run away?

I understand her, because I too know what it's like to have these demons you can't get away from. Listening to Emily speak, I feel as though I see a part of her. My heart aches at the pain on her face and tears beyond her eyes. She is hurting, but she masks it for everyone around her. She must do this to convince herself that she is okay, but I know that look when I see it. And she's not okay.

I flip my wrist and peer down at my watch. It's 8:08 am, and my body hurts. I have gone thirty hours without my drugs. Nausea engulfs my entire body into an almost unbearable sickness. I don't think I slept at all last night, but somehow, I made it here. Grandma would be happy for me.

As people talk about their stories, I begin to wonder if these stories will ever be me. A guy named Chad sitting directly across from me begins to talk. He has pin-straight blonde hair that falls onto his forehead, but he keeps pushing it off to the side with a head flip. He was born addicted to meth, and his mom was never able to stop after he was born.

He grew up experimenting and trying drugs at a young age. He doesn't blame his mom, though. By the way he talks about her, it sounds as though they have maybe come to terms with one another. Chad has been sober for nine and a half years. He's a twenty-something-year-old who did so much cocaine that he's followed by a cardiologist now.

It feels ridiculous to be here, but I told my mom I would come, so here I am. Since it's my first day, I don't feel obligated to discuss my life story to a room full of absolute strangers. I reassure myself that it's okay to just listen.

Mom has always believed I was too good for all the shit I put into my body. I ache with guilt because sometimes I think she blames herself for who I've become. I know she thinks there must have been something she could have done differently to make me turn out as a better son. Only I know there's nothing she could have done.

Her children have always been her number one priority, and I can remember her telling me that before she had kids, she always knew she was meant to be a mother. Intuition told her she would love to be a mother, to care for her children until they could care for themselves.

She always wanted to go back to school to study marine biology. She never found the time to because she was so involved with us kids growing up. To this day, she still has not gone back. She wants to make sure there's money for us to go to college if we choose to. I wonder if she will ever give herself a break and pursue what she wants to do.

When the meeting ends, I stand up and inhale a large, slow breath, before exhaling with relief that I can leave. The curly-haired girl stands before her chair and stares blankly at me, concluding with a smile before changing her gaze to the front door.

I follow her vast strides as she bolts toward the exit. Her legs are long and thin. She could be a model for all I know. She walks the opposite way of my house and crosses down over the town line. She must not live too far in the town over if she's walking here. I question if I should have offered her a ride home, but by the time I think of it, she's too far away to hear me. Why didn't I say something when I had the chance? I've never been slick with girls, so maybe this is a sign I would have created a disaster.

On my way home, I set my music on shuffle and an old Green Day song plays in my speakers. It sure reminds me of Jack. Once we had gotten our licenses, we would carpool to school and pretty much everywhere together. I miss him.

***

I woke up this morning thinking about my dad, who I now refer to as Ron. He doesn't deserve "Dad" as a title. Not anymore. Ron grew up in an old town in Arkansas where the grass grew thick, and you couldn't see civilization from the upstairs bedroom window.

He always bragged about how good my life was since I was taken care of by both my parents. His dad left his mom for another woman shortly after he started attending public school, and he didn't see much of him after that.

As I grew older, Ron's love for gin grew too and eventually topped the love he had for his children. The love he had for me. He routinely showed up late for baseball games and eventually stopped going altogether.

By the time high school graduation came around, I didn't even bother getting a ticket for him. He didn't ask why either. That's when I knew. Ron didn't care anymore, and I was okay with it because we had gotten used to living life without him.

Even though Ron chose booze over his family, I still love him. And I always forgive him. Because if I didn't, I would be a hypocrite. Here I am, fucked up, just like Ron.

Jack

I moved back north a few months ago and left behind everything and everyone. I didn't want to go. I had to. It was my choice, but at the same time, it wasn't. I wonder what I'd be doing had I stayed. Maybe things for Grayson would be a lot different if I was there with him.

I lay here on my cold sheets, alone, without anyone around to talk to. My room is a small square with no windows. Each wall is white and plain. Every day, this place seems to get smaller.

I'm starting to think I'm going crazy from talking to myself. I read an article once that it can be healthy to talk to yourself, mainly to express yourself through difficult things. So, I guess that's what I do. I talk until I feel better, then I wait to feel bad again and do it all over.

The lines on my forehead frown and my lips quiver as I sit here and reflect on my life. What are the things I regret? Dumb question. I regret everything that has brought me to where I am now. How did I let myself get here?

I miss the life I always knew growing up. The people. The buildings. The sunsets on dry summer nights when the mosquitoes aren't landing on your skin every minute, sucking your blood and leaving you itchy for days on end. I miss the warm air racing into my nostrils, keeping my entire body warm. Most of all, I miss the campfires and my best friend.

The town I lived in was small, but the people that lived in that town were what made it so alive. Everyone knew each other. Any given time you went out in public somewhere, you were bound to see someone you knew. Some people may think that's annoying to see people everywhere and have to converse. But it's something I look back on now and realize how much I miss it. I was very friendly with my classmates and all my neighbors. I enjoyed going out and seeing people that I hadn't seen in a while.

One of my neighbors, Mrs. Bailey, lost her husband to lung cancer about six or seven years ago. She had been living alone since then, taking care of herself and the house. All her children were living out on the west coast, so a visiting nurse had to show up once or twice a week.

About six months after living alone, she fell on her bathroom floor, breaking her right hip. She was in the hospital before going to a rehab center for what feels like more than enough time to heal. But then again, she's ninety-something years old. The first time I saw her at the grocery store after she had been discharged, she was so happy to see me. And to my surprise, I was pleased to see her.

She used to babysit me when I was little. She would take me to the pond at the end of the road in the winter. She taught me how to ice skate. I was instructed by her stern voice that you couldn't go out too far, or the ice would break. I learned that the hard way after not listening.

She always felt like family to me. She gave me comfort like she was my grandmother and I was her beloved grandson. I'm not sure if she had grandchildren of her own. I suppose her extra affection and time with me proved she didn't.

Throughout the years I always tried to help the Baileys. From time to time, I would mow their lawn and take their trash to the dump with my mom. The day that Mr. Bailey died, a part of Mrs. Bailey went with him. She isolated herself more, hid in her home, and only went outside to fetch the mail. Mrs. Bailey walked differently. And she sounded different. Her words were broken, and she faded into a different person.

I found out shortly after seeing Mrs. Bailey at the store that she had fallen again and broke a few more bones this time. I never suspected that that would be the last time I saw her out. She now lives in a nursing home alone without her husband, and without her trusty helper, me.

The neighborhood stayed alive after Mrs. Bailey left. A new family moved in— a mom, a dad, and twin boys who were a grade below me. I befriended them almost immediately. We met at the bus stop, which was across the street, equidistant from both of our houses. Grayson and the twins pretty much lived at my house up until I left and we went on our separate paths.

I lived in a small, blue ranch style home. My mom loved gardening, so most of the time our flowers were blooming in the soil she so very carefully tended to. I loved being outside and playing around barefoot. Most of my childhood I played in the one-acre back yard we had. I can remember my exact feelings when I played in that yard. It felt like I had a whole town worth of land that I could make my own. I reserved an area for a baseball field where I could hit balls on end and practiced for a career in baseball. Of course, that was before I realized later in life that that was not feasible. But I didn't know that then, and I don't regret having big dreams.

The entire yard was surrounded by a fence, which made it convenient for us to play with our dog outside and not worry about him running away the way he often did when he saw other animals, squirrels being a favorite of his.

The yard was almost entirely flat. A swing set stood tall to the far-right back corner and a sandbox laid in front of it. I begged Mom and Dad for an in-ground pool, but they told me that would be too expensive to put in and maintain. I settled for a five-hundred-gallon blow-up pool. Eventually, it stopped being fun as I outgrew it. It became a place where Mom would lay out on a floaty to keep fresh on a hot summer day and read her mystery novels.

Grayson and I have been best friends since the second grade. We met on the bus ride to school when I had recently moved to his neighborhood. I was the first stop, and he was the last. Kids were always taunting him because he cried one time when he missed his mom. He struggled to get on that bus every morning, in fear of peer rejection and not making any friends. Because who would want to be friends with a cry baby?

For weeks those ruthless little shits never left him alone. They called him names and threw spitballs at him. He sat next to me on the bus every day, and the kids finally stopped. Before I even told him my name, I nudged his shoulder with mine and said to him with a shy smile, "I miss my mom, too."

I still remember the first time Grayson came over my house and my mom made us chicken nuggets. We played outside for so long in the beaming sun that all our freckles came back to our faces in one day. Dirt covered the surface of our arms.

We used to build forts and pretend we lived outside and had to survive with the bare minimum. The pool was the ocean, where we fished for food that would keep us alive. The woods around us was the forest that we had to be wary of because of the wild animals that were vicious and hunters themselves.

One time in the seventh grade, we cut class together. It wasn't because we wanted to, but because everyone else had, so we wanted to be able to tell people that we had too. We just started switching classrooms every period at school, so we waited until after social studies so we could learn the countries and capitals of Africa, and then we hid out in the locker room and smoked weed. I will never forget that day because we got in so much trouble. It wasn't too funny then, but now I love telling that story.

Our friendship continued up through high school. We played baseball together every spring and drank on the beach all summer long. One of our buddies had a boat, and now and then we would water ski. Although, since we were amateurs, we would often fall more times than we were able to stand up. It wasn't until the next day that my throbbing legs revealed to me that I needed more muscle to handle an activity like that.

I always thought Grayson and I would be friends until we made it up to our 80s or 90s, but that's not how things worked out.

Emily

October has finally come, and I'll be two years sober on the seventeenth. What a fucking accomplishment. I never thought I would make it to this point—a point of freedom. If you had asked me five years ago where I would be today, I think I would have said that I'd be drinking throughout the day, telling everyone around me that I'm fine. But really, I'd have been alone and desperate. I know my mom would probably have hated me, and I would have no money. I would walk around, wondering where I would sleep or how I was going to eat.

But my mom couldn't have been more wrong about me, because here I am, still alone, making it by myself.

My first drink made my body so warm and numb. I felt like I could do anything. Little did I know I was going to rely on that feeling to get me through my days. After about four months of heavy drinking, I grew to be anorexic and was depleted of nutrition completely. I hardly ever ate or drank water. I would throw up all the time when I overindulged.

The bar was a good friend of mine, but I did a lot of drinking by myself in my room. Weekday, weekend, morning and night. All the time. Sleep was something I began to miss. I learned quickly that I only slept after some drinks.

I lived on the cusp of lifelong health issues and sickness. Who would I become? Would I die alone? I didn't think I could disappear from this battle. No one thinks that. We don't think it will ever be us until it is. And then, it's too fucking late.

When I died, I'd have a funeral with all my friends and some of my family in attendance crying because they couldn't help me no matter how much they tried or thought they could. Most of them wouldn't have seen me in a while because I barricaded myself, refusing to allow people into my life. Because the bottle was my real friend.

I don't know how my mom would react and feel planning her only child's funeral. Sad perhaps. Or maybe she'd feel relieved that it was over and she didn't have to deal with me anymore. I don't know. Perhaps I would be buried alone somewhere, and eventually I'd be forgotten, just like everyone else. But that's not how it went. Instead, I'm here. Alive.

It's 5:30 am, and I'm wide awake before my alarm is supposed to go off. I toss back and forth from my right side to my left, eventually turning to lay flat on my back. I stare at the white popcorn ceiling and begin to daydream. A few minutes pass when I look back at my clock, and I know I can't fall back asleep. I've been waking up at the same time every morning, no matter what time I fall asleep the night before, and my body isn't allowing me the courtesy of a day of sleeping in.

Just get up, I say in my head, persuading myself to start the day. I open my closet door and realize by the lack of clothes hanging that I had forgotten to go to the laundromat yesterday. I suppose I thought it wasn't at the top of the priority list. I quickly decide what to wear, not having many choices to begin with anyway. I put on some comfy black pants that appear to be of good quality, but they are stretchy and feel equivalent to pajama bottoms. I take the first sweater my hand touches, knowing anything will match. I comb my hair back into a ponytail to avoid any curls that may want to dangle on my face.

I stare at myself in the mirror, feeling like I look like a plain girl. But I suppose every girl must feel that way. No one thinks they are perfect.

I sit on the sofa in my five hundred square foot apartment that I just started renting a little over a month ago. I had been on my own for years, traveling from an unstable place to an unstable situation. At times, I stayed with friends. Others, I stayed in cheap motels that smelled like old cheese. This might be my stable place, right here. It's a place I call my own, and I don't have to worry about needing to move to another location soon. I've made it my sanctuary.

I've convinced myself that the situations I have been in are one hundred percent my fault and I try to not have any animosity toward my mom, who shut me out of her life completely and does not care about me anymore.

I don't know why. Maybe she hates the person I have become, or perhaps she hates herself for letting me get that bad. Either way, she doesn't give a shit, and there's nothing I can do to change that.

I step outside and fully embrace the fall beauty around me. The leaves are starting to make red and orange collages all around as the summer flowers wither away. I stare off for a moment, wishing nature would look this way all the time. I'm quickly frightened out of that fantasy and brought back to full awareness when a small Mercedes nearly runs me over going at least fifty miles per hour. *Asshole*, I note to myself, wishing that I had given the person the finger in time for them to see it.

The air is cool, but the sun shines, granting my skin some warmth as the trees sway in the breeze. Nature is beautiful. Walking to the meeting today sounds like a good idea to me. I walk over train tracks, bringing me back to senior year pictures. I loved the look of images with train tracks, and I always wanted to have my photo be there. So, when it came time, I had a friend take my pictures on the train tracks behind my mom's house.

I look at my watch and notice I've fallen behind time. Maybe I should've driven. I enter the doors, and everyone is already seated. I am not embarrassed to come late. Most days at least one person does the late stroll into the building. The only downside is that the door shuts loudly, and everyone glares as it echoes behind you.

He sits beside me in the circle with his head down staring at the hardwood beneath us, scuffed up from moving furniture and old age. His hair is light brown with one wave in it that starts where his part is and transforms into small curls at the edges. He looks up toward me as I sit down and right away, I'm stunned by his inquisitive blue eyes.

His shy face and minimal body gestures tell me this is his first time here, never mind the fact that I've never seen him before. I was the same way the first time. Curious and nervous about the unknown. Will this help me? Will I see someone I know? Will I be judged? My anxiety causes countless questions to form in my head during uncomfortable situations.

I've met some good friends here, but I'm curious to learn about him. Amy, a friend that I made on day one of my recovery, sits on the other side of him. She's ten years older than me and started drinking at fifteen. She has two young children who she recently regained custody of since proving her sobriety is being taken seriously.

I remember her introduction to me after my first meeting. Amy stood tall with a lean build and a pixie car cut. She wore 70's-style glasses and a jean satchel off her shoulder. Her voice was soft, and her words kind. I think she was indeed in need of a good friend and we became inseparable from that day on.

I think Amy would have lived a long, lonely life had she not gotten sober.

***

We're going out to dinner tonight because it's the only night she could get a sitter. I get dressed in jeans and a black shirt with a sunflower on it. My curls dangle on my shoulders tightly from the gel that's made each strand into a perfect circle.

I place a call to Amy to let her know I'm on the way to pick her up, but she does not answer. A minute or so later, she calls back. Loud, indistinctive voices in the background. She talks as though she must press her lips on the speaker for me to hear what she's saying. Surely, she couldn't be where I think she is. I stare down to the floor, picturing the last time I was there and heard that noise. It's too familiar to me not to know where Amy is. Before I can even ask where exactly she is, her voice gets louder, as if she doesn't want to answer the question she knows I am about to ask. Click. She's gone.

My phone lights up and dings, and I am almost afraid to look down at it. I peer with my eyes hesitantly, not turning my head downwards.

"Morgan's."

Is she fucking serious? The bar? After all this time and sacrifice? My eyes begin to water, and I question if I even really knew Amy or if it was all pretend. I worry that this may destroy my relationship with her because I can't turn back on that dark alley. I barely survived.

I wonder to myself why Amy would put me into this situation. Of course, I can't go there. Does she think I will meet her there instead of going out to dinner as planned? The overwhelming number of questions in my mind sends a shiver up my spine.

I will go and rescue Amy from her demons. I will knock sense into her stupid head, so she doesn't end up losing her kids. No. I will try. She needs to listen to me.

I start my car and drive almost all the way there before realizing I have been driving in complete silence, not touching the air temperature or the radio. I begin to sweat, not because I'm hot, but because of the confrontation that I fear will destroy a friendship that's made me who I am. And I don't want it to, but I need to face it to help Amy.

I must work up the courage to tell her she's out of her fucking mind, and hopefully she will understand my genuine intentions for barging into the bar.

I skim the people as my head turns in a panic. Before I can spot Amy, I see *her*. My mom. She stands straight, staring into my soul while shaking her head like I am a forever damaged girl. My body freezes and suddenly, I forget why I've even come here, but I know exactly what this looks like to her.

My feet anchor to the floor, and I try to turn away holding back my tears. I nearly trip as I bolt for the exit, catching myself on a stool before my face plants into the ground. I run to the parking lot without looking back, wishing I had never gone there in the first place.

Jack

My stomach is an empty pool of sadness that takes over my entire body, leaving me numb and helpless. Why does life have to be so cruel? I have had so much time to think about what I've done, but I don't know why this had to be me. Everyone makes mistakes, right?

The intensity of my flashbacks continues to grow, sending electric shocks from my head throughout my body, making the pain of my past unbearable. I must figure out a way to navigate out of this dark, agonizing spot I'm in.

But I don't know how. I want to be free. I want to move forward with whatever life I'm in now. But I'm stuck.

I now see myself for the ignorant, careless person I was. Grayson did these things. Not me. He always told me to never do what he did. I was too good for it. With my poor judgment, and the love I couldn't give to myself, I took a small white pill that would change everything for me. You see, I didn't do drugs. I drank away my pain and sorrows to help myself the only way I knew how to. It helped me breathe, sleep, and be normal until it couldn't help me anymore.

It has killed me watching Grayson kill himself. I have always wanted to save him. But now, I have failed. I had gotten to a place where I was so tired of being alive because I was dead inside. And the white pill came to my rescue, taking me out of my misery without even being asked to.

***

My screen moved quickly as I scrolled Facebook looking for pictures from the party I went to the week before. One picture in particular caught my eye that Grayson had uploaded. Why would he put this online? My eyes were squeezed together, and the relaxation on my face poses something for people to laugh at.

I lay on the green recliner that is partially tipped over from the lack of my weight where it's needed. Rather, I'm leaning toward the top with my arms dangling on each side of my body. I'm sure Grayson thought it would give people a good laugh. Jack the Beer Pong King, unconscious in the living room before the party was over.

Extreme embarrassment drenched my soul as I watched more and more people like the photo.

It's been online for ten hours. I could only imagine how many people had seen it. A mix of betrayal and anger boiled inside of me and I sat frozen in front of my computer, contemplating what to do.

Tom, my older cousin, sent me a message, and before I could open it, I could already read his words without even seeing them yet. I prayed he wasn't going to give me any shit. I knew he must have seen the photo.

"Yikes man." Just wonderful.

"Tell Gray to take that shit down man."

Obviously, that was my first thought I'm just so shocked it was put up online in the first place.

Tom and I talked for a few minutes. Growing up, we always went to family parties and hung out because most of my cousins were a lot younger than me, and I loved hanging out with someone older. Tom was a lot taller than me, and the first time I saw him with facial hair I remember thinking he looked so much older since the last time I saw him.

Every year when our family had Christmas parties at my grandmother's, Tom and I would eat until our stomachs blew up, then, we'd catch up with aunts and uncles we hadn't seen since the previous year. Green and red lights filled the kitchen and living room, and candles made the air you breathed a place you never wanted to leave.

The last Christmas party I went to, Tom said he had something planned for us. He told me to meet him near the basement door which was around the corner where all the cars were parked. At first, I thought he was mad at me or something. When I got there, I immediately felt like my bladder was going to explode. That feeling always happened to me when we were kids and played hide-and-go-seek. I would find the best hiding places, but as soon as I was settled, a nervous pee overwhelmed my body and I never knew if I would make it to the bathroom.

Tom greeted me with a backpack he pulled from around his shoulder. Alcohol. That's the big reason for meeting me here. He had somehow gotten a bottle and masterminded a plan to secretly drink it without our family noticing. That was the first time I had ever been drunk.

As I was about to close out Facebook, Tom sent another message. "Party here next weekend."

I suddenly doubted his invitation, given he had just seen my drinking outcome online. I can remember the excitement that never left my face for the days to follow. Out of everyone in the world, he chose me. He must have thought I was cool enough for a college party or else he wouldn't have brought the idea up to me. It made me giddy, and I thought this would prepare me for my future college life.

It was a party I bragged about up until the day came for us to pack the truck and leave town for the weekend. Grayson wanted to go, but I was still pissed off at him and Tom said he didn't want to wind up babysitting teenagers anyways. One was more than enough, he insisted.

I was too comfortable lying to my mom. Of course, I had done it before when I hung out with girls or went to parties in town, although I think in the back of her head she always knew. And the truth is, I often spent a lot of time with friends after school and especially on weekends so technically I was only half lying.

I packed my backpack full of clothes and a toothbrush. My mom didn't ask twice about where I was going. Sometimes I wish she would have.

I was ready to go two hours before Tom was supposed to pick me up, and at that time, I imagined what I'd be like as a college student living on campus with a bunch of people my own age and not having a curfew. I could go anywhere I wanted and didn't have to report off to Mom every time I left my dorm.

I threw my stuff in the back seat where handles of Smirnoff and Myer's lay on the floor, semi-covered with pieces of clothing. Tom was only twenty at the time. He probably asked a stranger at the liquor store to buy him stuff. That's what he usually did. I didn't ask though. It didn't matter as long as we got the booze. He saw my eyes wander to the sleeve of nips tucked into the backseat pocket. I'm not sure what my face looked like, but he told me to shut my mouth as I looked back toward him.

We drove to his school about two hours away from my house. The entire car ride I was so excited, but nervous at the same time. This was my first time going to a college party. Would people know I was a high schooler? I wasn't sure what college parties were like, other than what I saw in movies, but I didn't know if those were accurate.

Highschool parties that I knew were nothing crazy—a bunch of people squashed into the kitchen and living room—loud music. People talking in circles and drinking beer. I wonder if it will be the type of party where people get so messed up, they do somersaults off of the roof and into the pool. Are there pools at college? I'm not too sure, but I think of all types of scenarios I might be in and try to maintain my calm.

Once we settled in Tom's dorm, we walked a few blocks down the street to his friend's rental house. That's where we started pre-gaming, a term I learned that night. A concept that you go somewhere for a smaller party to get drunk enough to show up to the real party.

The pre-gaming house looked like it was run by a bunch of negligent young adults who were unaware that dump stickers existed. Trash was scattered through the yard, and beer cans sat empty around the front steps. As we walked through the front door, the air smelt of dirty dishes and stale pizza. The floor was hardwood but in terrible condition. Dried up liquor masked the floorboards and my sneakers stuck to them with every step.

We played every game imaginable for a group of college kids to play— pong, kings, flip cup. With every sip I took, I wondered how these guys lived this kind of lifestyle multiple days of the week. I assumed everyone there was a student. Where would they have found the time to be diligent with schoolwork or even work a job? These questions made me even a little worried to go to college in the future. It was obviously a busy life to maintain. Especially if I wanted to be like those guys there.

As our round of flip cup ended, one of Tom's friend pulled out a small white baggie from his back pocket, something I had never actually seen in person before. That would be my first day and my last day trying drugs.

Grayson

Ron gave me my first sip of beer when I was thirteen. The sizzling yellow glass smelled of old tree bark and I scrunched my nose as soon as the smell entered my nostrils.

"Don't be a pussy," Ron said to me, nearly attacking his own son with such adult words. "You have to try it."

The beer entered my throat, burning its entire way into my stomach. The aftertaste stayed only a day and then disappeared, same as Ron.

***

Today is just one of those days when I feel lonely and can't seem to bring myself to talk about why. Maybe it is that I don't really have anyone to talk to. Jack is gone. And I'm entangled with such severe sadness that I don't think I can move. This must be what rock bottom feels like— wanting to go out and do something to change, but giving myself enough reasons to stay right where I am.

My mom invites herself into my room unannounced, probably because she has not heard me make a sound since last night. I want to lay here, in this exact position, for the rest of the year. I ignore her words, focusing on the aching pain on the right side of my chest from my anxiety. She leaves in silence, only making a small creak as she shuts the door behind her.

By now, I've had enough panic attacks that mimic a heart attack that it doesn't scare me anymore. If Ron has passed down his high cholesterol to me, I'm already prepared for the worst.

I lay flat on my back, staring at the popcorn ceiling that begins to look smoother the longer I stare. I don't think I've blinked for a solid thirty seconds. My eyes slowly cross toward my nose and begin to close with ease.

I'm reminded by Jack that I am in complete control of what happens in my life. I decide what happens to me. Only I can change who I will be in the future.

I stand from my bed, ignoring the vertigo that is taking over my body, deciding at this very moment that I will push myself to do something. *Baby steps*, I tell myself. Just go do something, anything.

I head into a shopping area in town that has a four-mile bike path behind a coffee shop I used to go to before school. The path is known for the bridges and streams. I've heard people even go horseback riding down there. I pull into the parking space furthest from the building, noticing immediately this is a completely different coffee shop from the last time I was here.

The building has been repainted a faint pink. Nothing too bright to scare someone away, but pink enough to stand out from the other white and brown buildings. Coffee and muffin decorations sit in the windows and a person dressed up in an espresso costume stands outside the main entrance. I can't help but laugh to myself. I've seen a lot of advertising with costumes before, but this one just looks absurd.

The poor kid in the suit can't be older than sixteen. He probably just found some bullshit job to make his mom happy. There's no way he wanted to do what he's doing. I try to strike up a conversation, but he's too embarrassed to look me in the eye. I bet he's hoping no one from school shows up here, knowing he would be teased for having the stupidest job in the world. But I applaud him. At least he's doing something. He sure is doing a hell of a lot more than me.

My stomach begins to growl, followed by a burning sensation, reminding me that I haven't eaten anything all day. I open the door to walk in, but before I can fully get my body through the doorway, I see her — the curly-haired girl. I stop where I'm standing as I stare, not caring about browsing the menu as I had seconds ago.

She sits at a large table as if she is expecting company, but instead pulls out her laptop and a few folders with a matching purple notebook. She neatly organizes her things on the table, not wasting an inch of the surface. She must have a lot planned. She can't be meeting people here. Maybe she is studying for a test.

The smell of pancakes fills my nose and carries into my lungs, and I exhale with a large sigh. My mouth begins to water as I imagine devouring chocolate chip pancakes that my mom used to make me before school when I was little. This place is heavenly.

Emily—I think her name is. She looks about my age, early to mid-twenties. As she catches my eyes on her, I start to walk in her direction, unsure if I should walk past her or stop to say something.

She's even more beautiful than I had remembered. She looks at me with a half-smile, giving me hope that she recognizes me from the meeting. Or, she thinks I'm a complete freak who's staring at her. As I get closer, it becomes apparent she remembers me when she starts to signal me with her hand to sit down across from her at the table.

"I'm Emily," she says. I smile as the words "curly-haired girl" come racing past my lips.

She smiles back, and for a second, I question why the hell I just said that out loud. At this point, I am positive this girl will never talk to me again.

To my surprise, she invites me to sit with her, and I'm suddenly nervous, biting my bottom lip, praying I don't choke up and say something stupid. This is something I often did in high school before I had to get up in front of a room full of classmates and do a presentation.

I know this isn't a date, but as I gaze at her across the table, I'm embarrassed because I realize I haven't told her my name. I introduce myself and ask her what all the papers are for.

"I'm enrolled in a creative writing class," she tells me. "I have been writing poetry for a little while, and I thought I could benefit from taking a class or two."

She explains to me with great certainty that she will write a book of her own someday, at least, once she has everything figured out. She works full time and has an apartment she's been renting. Now I remember her saying something back in the meeting about her mom. Emily must still be on her own.

"So, what about you?" she inquires, genuinely interested in what I'm about.

I tell her about my struggles with addiction and how it kills my mom every day. Growing up, she and I were very close, and everyone could tell by the way I acted that I was her son.

Throughout our whole conversation, it is evident that Emily relates to my hardships and sorrows during the last few years. She places her hand over mine, and for a minute, we sit in silence. "I understand what it's like. You will be okay, you know," she says, assuring me of my very own desire of being clean and sober someday.

For one reason or another, I believe her words. The way they roll off her tongue sends me a promise of hope, and I begin to wonder what my life would be like if I didn't do drugs. It's hard to think about actually, because it is part of who I am now, and it's difficult to remember life without them. Or maybe I choose not to remember. I am suppressing memories that hurt so much now because I'm not that person anymore.

Emily is full of courage and ambition, something I too would like to achieve when I'm ready to be clean. But I don't know if I'm there yet like she is. She carries herself with confidence and is sure what her goals and dreams are. I begin to wonder what it was for her to make this drastic change. How did she completely turn her life around, and what do I have to do to have that too?

My butt begins to vibrate, and I pull my phone from my back pocket. I realize I have been sitting here with Emily for nearly three hours now talking. "I'm sorry, I have to go."

Emily

My drinking nearly killed me. Death had invited me to its doorsteps, almost taking me inside while closing the door behind me, forbidding me to leave.

I had been sitting in my Honda in my parent's driveway. I don't know how long I was there for—minutes, maybe hours. It was long enough to alarm them when they realized I didn't make it through the front door.

I woke up in the hospital, seeing people in blue scrubs and white lab coats pass up and down the hallways. Fear coated my skin as I sat there not able to recollect how I had gotten there. Or what I did to get there. Alone, and in a panic, I started to cry uncontrollably, imagining that I may have hurt someone else. I just didn't know. Did I get into a car accident?

I didn't even think I was at the bar for that long. The last thing I remembered was eating oyster crackers and having a drink with the tall guy who was sitting next to me. I remembered his face, which was much older than mine, flirting with me nonstop until I felt uncomfortable and violated in a way. After that, I don't remember a thing.

The moments I waited for someone to enter the room and tell me what had happened soon turned into minutes, which felt like hours. There was no information in the room. A computer hung off the wall and next to it a whiteboard, that showed the name of my nurse.

They told me I fell asleep reclined in the driver's seat while intoxicated. I then vomited which caused me to choke and aspirate my vomit. My admission to the hospital was only the beginning. They diagnosed me with aspiration pneumonia and alcohol withdrawal. I was given tons of Ativan to help with my withdrawal symptoms, not that I wasn't going to drink once I was discharged home.

Mom didn't let me come back home, though. I think that event was a realization she had slowly come to, that she may indeed have to bury me one day. I believed that she was angry with me and couldn't stand to watch me slowly kill myself. She would never understand.

***

The bell rings twice as the glass door swings open and lets in a gust of humid, garbage smelling air. I think it often smells like that around here because of all the people coming and going throughout this part of town. This place is so dirty. Nevertheless, this is the place that saved me.

I've been working at this bookstore since I became sober. With clear thoughts and better nights of sleep, I learned so much about myself. Every single day I would read a lot of paranormal romance books. Then, I started writing poems and short stories. Whatever inspired me, I put on paper.

My boss Glen has been so supportive throughout my recovery. He's exactly how I wish my mom were to me. Glen had a daughter

Miranda who died last year. She was an alcoholic who drove herself to her end.

Miranda got off work early one night and went to the bar where she was well known and often had dinner. It never crossed her mind that she would wrap herself around a telephone pole that night.

I often wonder if Glen treats me the way he does because of Miranda. He's understanding and supportive in a way that's not overbearing like a non-stop worried parent. Maybe he sees that I am the fucked-up girl who has managed to turn her life around. Maybe he is happy for me.

But maybe, somewhere deep down, he's inconsolable, knowing Miranda never got that chance to change.

6 Weeks Later

Emily

He's awkward, but weirdly, it's cute. I don't know if he's dated a lot, but it doesn't freak me out. He's sweet. Grayson and I have been spending time together nearly every day of the week. When we're not together, we're texting nonstop or facetiming. We've become this inseparable pair that doesn't get sick of each other.

Last weekend he took me horseback riding. It's not the typical time of year to do something like that considering the ground is frozen hard and we could see our breath. The trail was so peaceful. Trees were in the process of becoming naked of leaves, which left the sun's rays to pass through each branch, allowing us some warmth. This place would be like a landmark for me.

We shared our first kiss there and when our flesh touched, I thought my stomach was going to burst into a million pieces. Happiness filled my veins, and my heart burned with love. Maybe it's not love. But is it too soon? No. Perhaps, it is love.

***

Grayson's coming over to my apartment for the very first time and although I know he wouldn't care if things were messy, I feel the need to perfect everything around it. I start cleaning from top to bottom, sanitizing everything that I can spray and wipe down. I'm worried by the old style of this place. Nothing ever appears clean. Grime shows in the lines between the tiled floor no matter how hard I scrub. There's a red stain in front of the kitchen sink from previous renters that bleach cannot restore. The only solution is to get new floors.

I organize all my mail and letters I've written but have yet to send.

Dear Mom,
I'm sorry for everything.
I miss you and hope that one
day you will forgive me and
I can hug you again. Stay well.
Emily

I've written several letters like this. Once I've composed them, I stare at each word, fearing the reaction my mom might have when she opens a letter and reads the plea of her unforgivable daughter. I try to imagine her face—confused and hateful. I wonder if she'd write back or maybe try calling me, or if she would throw it in the trash and forget she even read it to begin with.

I wish that she wanted to be here with me to watch me rise. She only knows the old Emily. She has cheated herself out of getting to know the real me—the happy, stable, and sober me.

But I suppose I should stop enduring the guilt that I have created myself. Somehow, I must learn to give myself a break sometimes. The guilt has eaten away at my body, leaving me emotionally torn. It's past due for me to let go of things that I cannot change—*people* I cannot change.

My mom chose to watch me fall and did not care enough to watch me get back up. But that was her decision. All I can do now is be the best version of me that I know how to, although it pains me to do so without her. I lived for so long furious at her, but I think I have surpassed that stage of grief. Now, it's just sad to think about.

It's always been a dream of mine to have my perfect wedding someday. Oddly enough, I still include my mom when I envision the ceremony. She has yet to leave my visions of the future, although she has already left my life in the present.

I don't recall when our last conversation was, or what we talked about. I wonder if one day she will ever want to be a grandmother to my children and see them grow up. I wonder if she'll care for them, even though she doesn't care for me. Or will she reject them like she has rejected me all this time?

The oven timer sounds and the sweet smell of banana bread fills the room as I place it on the stove to cool. It is a sacred recipe I learned from my mom when I was young, and it stays engraved in my brain.

I suggest to Grayson that he come over soon so we can order Chinese and eat the bread while it's still warm. I can see he has read my message, but he has not responded yet.

By the consistency and depth of our conversations, I'm starting to notice a genuine, raw connection that we share. When I say raw, I mean that we don't need to be doing anything special to have fun and enjoy each other. When I'm with Grayson, I don't feel nervous anymore. I don't feel the sadness of family betrayal and loss. He makes me feel at home.

We are very similar too—we've both struggled with an addiction that has destroyed so many relationships around us. We know what it's like to ruin someone else's life because we can't keep ourselves together.

But I'm okay now. And so is Grayson. He seems a lot happier since I met him—or at least that's what his mom has told me. She says that Grayson has made his way out of his room for longer periods during the day and is always excited to see me again.

Her words give me a relieving validation that my feelings for Grayson are one hundred percent reciprocated. I can't imagine spending my time with anyone else besides him. He's been clean, and I am satisfied with how far we've both come. We are right for each other.

He gets to my apartment, and our Chinese food gets delivered right as he's walking in. *Perfect timing*, I think to myself.

Grayson looks tired today, but I don't bother to ask what's wrong because I think I already know. He knows I know. His head stays down, avoiding any eye contact with me. He's kind of quiet, whereas usually, we talk nonstop.

We eat our food in silence, and I'm pondering the thought of asking him if he's okay, but I don't want to trigger him. I've often hated when people would ask me that question, but never realized I ask it just as much as everyone else. For some reason, when people would ask if I'm alright, it only heightened my emotions and made me angry with the person who so stupidly asked very well knowing I was not alright.

I suggest we watch a movie, an activity that doesn't involve us looking at each other or talking for that matter. We get to the movie's halfway mark when Grayson places his hand on mine and faces me with his tired, sad eyes. At this moment, I have confirmation.

He's using again.

Tears start to drip down his cheeks, and we sit in silence as I hold him in my lap. It feels like we have been in this position forever, but his grip on my arm begs me not to let go.

Grayson

The sound of rap music rings in my ears so loud I feel like I'm on a never-ending roller coaster. I'm screaming and using all the air in my lungs, but still, no one can hear me. My voice shrieks as I beg for someone to help me, but I'm afraid that there is no one around to hear me.

This perpetual craving started when I began smoking weed at fourteen. It made me happy until someone introduced me to heroin, which made me even happier.

I was at a bonfire with Jack and a few other friends from the neighborhood one night. We made a trail out to the middle of the woods and agreed that's where we'd party. Even in the dead of winter, we would party in twenty-three degrees. Some unfamiliar people had shown up, but we didn't care. Everyone got along pretty well, and we never really found out how they heard about the fire we were having.

This is the night the brown powder took over my life. Tyler, one of the new kids who showed up that night, offered some to me. I don't know why, but I didn't hesitate to say yes. And Tyler became my new best friend.

***

I'm thinking of Emily. I want to pull her close to me as I cup my hand on her silky cheek, kissing her softly. Our bodies fit together like we are made to hold one another. Her hair is so soft that each strand separates through my fingers as I run my hand toward the back of her head. I love her, but I'm not sure if she knows it.

I'm feeling something I've never thought about feeling toward someone. The one meeting I did go to—led to her. I love the way her hair blows in the wind and her skin glows as we say goodbye to the sun. Even as it has gotten cooler, we still manage to have our dates to watch the sunsets. She looks like a girl that should be in a movie.

I take it all in for a moment. Grateful that out of all the people out there, she has chosen me. But I don't deserve her. I wish she was here with me right now.

I'm shaking so intensely, that the few hairs dangling on my forehead begin to tickle my skin with rage. I can hear my mom yelling that dinner is almost ready as what seems like puddles of cold sweat drips down my temples. I hold my knees up to my chest with my arms wrapped around my legs so tight that I feel like I'm going to stop breathing any minute now. I pray my mom does not walk into my room as I do the one thing she cannot bear to know.

Tears pour down my cheeks and I press my lips shut, despising the dreadful taste of salt. *This is the last time*, I say, but I don't even know if I can fucking believe myself anymore. I'm no good for Emily if I can't be who she needs me to be. She got her shit together, and I'm not going to screw that up for her. People are proud of her. They don't need some guy coming into her life to put her back to square one. And neither does she.

I am proving myself a failure. I am living a life like Ron. Although unlike him, my heart knows this is all wrong and I am not supposed to be this person. I'm sure Ron wouldn't be surprised if he knew how I turned out. And I bet he wouldn't think there was anything wrong with it either. His moral compass points to whatever the hell he feels like doing—right or wrong.

I'm sitting on my bedroom floor right next to the stain where I spilled hot chocolate when I was eleven. I think back to those days, a time when I wasn't wondering about the next time that I could get high.

Jack would come over after school and we would play video games until my mom called us for dinner. We created screennames, so we could instant message our friends before we had cell phones. Those were the good days. I don't know if good days will ever come back to me.

I have everything I need right in front of me. All I have to do is stick that syringe in my vein, and everything will feel all better. I could do this whole sobriety thing but fuck, I can't bear to feel this pain any longer. As bad as it sounds, the choice between this and Emily is quite easy for me to make.

As the sunshine flows through my veins, I can't help but feel a moment of peace. Everything around me is still, and I'm comforted by the silence. I close my eyes as I fall into a deep relaxation, yet I am able to open my eyes to Emily's phone call.

As my words flow slowly, I'm suddenly distracted by a brightness above me and a person walking toward me with a graceful approach. I reach my arm out with great desperation as my hand impatiently waits for Jack to extend his back toward me.

This is the first time I have seen Jack since he was alive.

Jack

Grayson sits below me on the futon in his bedroom. I can remember playing video games and eating chips on that exact piece of furniture that has now evolved into something much more dangerous. It would be the place where he lays unconscious while his breaths slowly cease.

The room is dim, and his mom calls out for him once again to get downstairs before his plate is cold. She has no idea. As she prepares food for everyone, her son lays limp, dying in the upstairs bedroom of their home. I want her to go upstairs to get him, for she is his only immediate hope. She can help him, but she does not think to bother him and so he remains alone in his room. I've been keeping my eye on him for this very reason.

***

Grayson debates his agenda tonight. I watch him question himself—his life. The thought of drugs swarms his mind like hundreds of angry bees circling his head, refusing to fly away. He screams angrily at himself as he uses open palms to smack his face, trying to wake himself up from this nightmare. But his ordeal is real life. And he does it again.

I thought that after I died, Grayson would want to honor me in a way that meant he had to stop doing drugs. He doesn't realize that he could die. He doesn't think it will ever be him. But of course, I know it can because it happened to me. And it only took one time for me to go into cardiac arrest, ending my life.

I don't know why he does this to himself. I looked up to him like he was my big brother. I thought he would be someone special one day. But since losing me, I think he has stopped caring about trying to get better and has instead focused on his temporary fix to feel better.

He grew sad and depressed, but once he met Emily things changed. Or at least, I thought they were going to. I thought that him meeting someone like her would influence him to change. I do think he tried. But it's difficult for him. He has battled this for too long.

He starts to nod off, but his phone rings, alarming him as his eyes close fully. It's Emily. He answers and is somewhat coherent. She thinks she just woke him up, but only I know the truth at this very moment.

They exchange a few words with each other, and the call ends abruptly. The last thing Grayson tells her she can barely comprehend. His speech grows slow and slurred, and eventually dissipates into silence.

Emily is a smart girl. I need her to know what he has done, or he will die. And I don't want him coming here with me. I want to stay here alone. I want to continue to watch Grayson try to fix his life and hopefully see him grow old. I'm okay with being here alone.

Grayson lays there, nearly lifeless. His skin cold, his color starts to lighten. His heart, getting mixed signals from his brain, starts to beat irregularly and eventually begins to slow.

He lays there alone. But he is not alone, because I am here, and I am not letting him die. And I hope Emily won't either.

For the love of Grayson, I look over him and try to help from afar, but he does not hear my soundless voice. My voice is roaring louder and louder. I cry out to Grayson. If my heart stilled worked, it would be pounding through my chest. He can't do this to himself. Not now, and not ever.

There is a permanent wall between us that has cut off all communication, and for that, I sob because I cannot save him. I could not even save myself. I fall to my knees as I yell to God to let him stay, begging Him not to let this be his last day. Emily needs to save him.

Grayson looks up right at me and I plead for him to go back to her.

She is coming.

Emily

I drop my phone before hanging up, in disbelief of the voice I just heard over the phone. My phone lands screen side down on the hard floor. With the sound of glass shattering, pieces dart across each square tile in the kitchen. Grayson's speech was garbled. He told me he loves me but said nothing else. And that was when I knew. I'm frozen where I stand, and my throat is too dry for me to scream.

My blood boils with panic, and I start to shake uncontrollably. I feel my head pulsating, ready to burst open into a million pieces. A cold sweat forms on my forehead just on the edge of my hairline.

My heart drops into my stomach and sits there. I cry out in physical pain. I hold my stomach and drop to my knees as the pain shoots down into my lower back before making its way down my legs.

For a moment, I'm preoccupied with the agony that has taken over my body. I never knew I could feel like this. How is it possible to find out something so terrible? The pain attaches itself to my body, leaving me unable to walk or even think.

The room appears to be closing in toward me, suffocating my chest, and I am unable to inhale. I have a flashback of one of my favorite dates with Grayson. We went to a carnival taking place right on the beach. We stayed out all night, laying on a small beach blanket together. We never slept. All night we talked about our future and what things would be like.

The absence of my breathing alerts my brain, and I gasp for air as I start to get dizzy, realizing I need to go. And I need to go quick. My legs tumble over each other as I try to gather my things. I search for not even five seconds and notice I am losing time.

I run to my car with no shoes or wallet. I wish I weren't hysterically crying right now because I know this will only slow my driving down. I put the key into the ignition, but the car doesn't start. I feel a shot of adrenaline shoot through the veins in my arms when I realize I am putting the wrong key in.

I scream to myself, hitting my palms on the steering wheel. But I have no business wasting time. I need to get my shit together and go. I can't have any distractions if I want to save him—not even by my emotions.

My eyes bleed with tears making it even more difficult to focus on the dark road ahead of me. I'm going fifteen miles per hour over the speed limit and I don't care if the cops see me. This is an emergency and they can chase me if they want, but I'm not pulling over.

The sound of raindrops hit the windshield and the noise pounds in my ears. My windshield wipers make a scratchy noise as they go back and forth, not cleaning the rain entirely off the glass. The commute to Grayson's turns into what feels like a trip around the country.

I watch the clock as the minutes go by. I'm wishing I could freeze time because even though I'm driving fast, I may be too late. But I can't be too late. This is unfair. He won't have the chance to get better, and I know in his heart he wants to be better. I pray to God I make it to him in time.

As I approach his house, his driveway is full, and without even questioning it, I pull onto his front lawn and throw my car into park. I don't shut the driver's door. That's another second of energy I waste on something that isn't Grayson.

I enter the house, screaming out for him, huffing and puffing while trying to say something to his mom. It's like I've just ruined dinner time at their house. Everything was quiet until I came roaring in like a maniac. His mom, in fright of my loud cry, follows me as I run up the stairs to Grayson's room.

I jerk his bedroom door open, afraid of what I will see on the other side. Grayson lays motionless, his breathing shallow and barely present at all. I yell at him, and he does not respond. I fall to the ground, paralyzed by what I see and struggle to get to my feet. I crawl to him with tears bursting out of my eyes like fireworks. I hold my hands on his cheeks and lean forward to him without releasing my lips from his skin.

His mom has already called 911, and we wait for what seems like forever for the paramedics to arrive. *He is alive*, I remind myself.

The only thing I can think of right now is what will happen if I lose Grayson. How will I be able to carry on after holding the person I love while he fades away in my arms? What will happen to his mom—the woman who would die just so Grayson could live one more day on Earth.

I hear the sirens approach and I'm finally able to take a satisfying breath in. It's the first time I've felt any sort of relief since that devastating phone call.

As soon as my hope rises, it's quickly destroyed when I no longer feel Grayson's chest rising. I scream at God to give him back. Grayson's mom is hyperventilating behind me as she watches her son die right in front of her. I feel as if a large glass window has fallen on my body and torn all my skin off, leaving my insides exposed and vulnerable.

As I start chest compressions, the ambulance lights peer through the window and reflect against the wall I'm facing.

Finally. Grayson is taken away on a stretcher, while the paramedics simultaneously try to revive him in time to save his life.

I am left in deep awe, not knowing if the love of my life is going to survive.

Grayson

The bright light above wakens me to a deep and uncomfortable panic. I know this lighting. Fluorescent. It's white and revealing, beaming down without any warmth. It's cold and without a soul. This lighting is a sign to me that I'm fucked.

But I'm alive.

I wiggle my fingers as I bite my lower lip, curious to know what hospital I've gotten myself admitted to this time. My bed lays at one hundred and eighty degrees, and I find myself too weak to sit myself up on my own. All parts of me are absent in this room. I wear a hospital gown, and I'm sure my phone is not here. I feel like an intruder here, like I need to get up quickly and sneak out before anyone notices me.

I wonder if my mom knows I'm here. But more importantly, does Emily? Does she know what I've done? I worry that this will permanently end us, because I never actually said the specific words to her that I had been using again.

I regret not telling her, because after all, she is my best friend. She is the one person I have been leaning on. I guess I couldn't bring myself to tell her that the worst habit of my life had returned.

But all along, I think Emily had to know. She must have known and not wanted to ask me because she didn't want to hear the answer out loud.

I feel like I am torturing her and fucking with her head. Everything was truly perfect with her and I have been falling for her, but I've also fallen for my worst enemy.

A woman walks into my room and stands at the left side of my bed. Before she introduces herself, I imagine that she is my nurse. She wears solid green scrubs and a stethoscope around her neck. Her skin is pale she's almost see-through. Her veins show in her face, but her skin is immaculate. She has no freckles or blemishes. She is pretty, but her features prove she is way too young to be a doctor. As she nears, I can read her name tag—Misty Brown, Registered Nurse.

She asks me how I am feeling, her words sincere. She explains what's going on with my body. My chest is covered with sticky circles, which serve a purpose to monitor my heart. I've been given doses of Ativan for seizure activity. She concludes with the question I was hoping she wouldn't bother to ask.

"Do you know what happened that brought you here?"

Of course, I know what brought me here. I raise my eyebrows with the intention of giving her a sarcastic look and she hears my silent response, not repeating the question. She lowers her head with a quiet nod and leaves the room heading for the nurse's station.

I sit here alone, trapped by my thoughts. I hope that Emily forgives me and understands. But I am prepared for the worst. Or at least, I think I am.

She may want to delete me from her life. What if she's so angry she can't talk to me? I don't know what I'd do. I'm so overwhelmed with thinking about her, I realize I should have asked the nurse if I could call my mom. Maybe there's a phone next to the bed, but I can't see. I lay flat on my back feeling defeated.

A single tear leaves my eye and I lay there staring at the ceiling. I am ruining my life.

My mother walks in several minutes after Misty has been gone. Her face is red and filled with tears. She hugs me and begins a loud cry. I can hear someone shut the door behind her. Her head aside mine, she cries over my shoulder, begging me, "Please Grayson. Please stop this."

My face fills with blood, and my scalp grows hot with sweat. I begin to cry uncontrollably as my mother's head slides down to my chest. I hold her tight, knowing how much it kills her to see me like this. An addict—her son who she hopes won't leave this earth before her, and yet, she prepares herself every time she gets a call that I'm in this place, unaware of the severity.

She has been in the hospital since I arrived and hasn't left my side. I learn that I have been unconscious for eighteen hours. I've required close monitoring because of arrhythmias, which is a fancy word for abnormal heart rhythms. I have IV's in both arms. I'm getting pumped with drugs for my heart along with hydration.

I feel like shit. I ask my mom if Emily knows what has happened. She is quiet for a moment, in deep thought, contemplating how to tell me. She looks nervous. It's a face I've never seen on her before. And that freaks me out.

"Mom!" I yell at her, begging her to just give me the fucking answer that I know she is having a hard time saying. I need to know. Doesn't she understand that?

"Gray," she says to me, her voice cracking as if she has no voice left to give me. She exhales as the words begin to trickle off her tongue.

"Emily...she's the one who found you."

Emily

He has broken me.

But why did I think an addict could change for another person in recovery? What possessed me to think Grayson would break a terrible addiction for me? That would be too good to be true.

I am foolish. Shit isn't that simple, but I wish it were. Of course I suspected something like this could happen, but my hope overshot my doubt, and now I am left broken and defeated. No, I didn't think I could change him. I just hoped he would want to change for me.

Part of my heart bears guilt. I knew that day at my apartment what he had been doing. Why did I not offer to help? Or at least offer a person that could listen to him—to his feelings or whatever he felt like he needed to say.

As I sit at my kitchen table, nerves wrap themselves around every inch of my body at the thought of seeing Grayson again. This is the first time I have felt this way by just thinking about him.

This feeling is concerning to me. It's crazy how I can feel one way, but then, just over a few days, all my feelings could change. I still love Grayson, but I fear for the success of our relationship together. I don't know if we will make it.

My phone lights up as I get a text message from Corrine, Grayson's mom.

"He's awake."

My heart is happy for a split second, reminding me how grateful I should be that he is okay. He is alive. As nervous as I am to see him, it's all I want to do. I quickly get ready and head over to the hospital.

I can't believe this is happening again. I am reluctant to walk into Grayson's room, not because I don't want to see him, but because I don't want to relive that part of my life again.

The hospital beds, the doctors—it's all overwhelming.

This stress is bringing me back in time, and I fight the feelings of when I had to climb out of my deep, dark hole. The temptation to drink will never dissipate, but now I have a better sense of redirecting myself into healthier habits.

Poetry has become a hobby of mine. At times when I feel so low and I think of drinking, I write everything down. My struggles, my feelings, my hopes. I have four notebooks that I have filled during the past two years of my sobriety.

I had been doing so well. I sustained wounds on my heart as I watched someone I genuinely care about nearly get himself killed.

As I approach room 524, Grayson's Mom turns around and signals a "be quiet" gesture with her finger over her lips. She gets up and walks over to me, so I've barely crossed the doorway and made it into the room.

"He just fell back asleep. You sit. I'm going to go get some food." She places her hand on my shoulder and smiles sadly as she exits the room. She has brought him sunflowers that sit near the far end of the bedside table next to the window.

I walk toward the blue chair that sits next to Grayson's bed. I stand in between the chair and bed, staring over Grayson's sleeping body. His respirations are calm.

I place my hand on his knee, blankets separating our skin. My palm shifts back and forth along with the sheet, soft enough not to wake him but enough pressure that it feels comforting— comforting for me.

But how does Grayson comfort me? I dream of having a family one day. Maybe two or three kids with a husband I love beyond belief. I need someone who I can care for and comfort during the hard times, and I need those actions to be reciprocated. Could he ever be this person I so much long for? The more I think about it, the less I think it could be Grayson.

I can't help but wonder if he will ever get better. I wonder if he will ever be clean so that he and I can continue to build each other up and start over again. I ponder this thought, and instead of thinking of a better life for us, I begin to lose hope. Tears stream down my face, and I don't think I can help him anymore. My mom's voice echoes through my ears, *we can only help ourselves*.

The room is almost too bright, and I question how he has stayed asleep this long. He must be so tired. I can remember when I would sleep twelve to sixteen hours at a time, only getting up to use the bathroom or take a sip of water.

He wakes up ten minutes or so after I've sat down. He gazes over to me with happiness, and his facial expression shows that he has missed me. I can't hide my disappointment. My eyebrows are raised, creating sad wrinkles on my forehead. And I don't smile.

Grayson has never judged me. So why is it so easy for me to judge him? I can't judge him. I have been here before, literally.

I'm angry with myself. Why the hell am I acting like this? I've been in his exact place wishing someone would be on my side and not ridicule me for my mistakes.

I have become the biggest fucking hypocrite.

Grayson

I turn my head to the right where my beautiful girl sits next to me. I can't imagine what this has done to her. I don't think there are enough words in the world for her to understand how truly sorry I am. I don't know at this moment what's going through her mind, but I am eager to hear her even though I fear her words.

Her face reveals deep sadness. I'm sure I have scared the living shit out of her. How did she know to come for me? I don't dare to ask because I am ashamed. I am just grateful she came when I needed her. That's what we have each other for, right?

How could I put her in this position? I didn't intentionally do it, but I should have known it would come to this. Sooner or later, I would put us in this situation. I wish I wasn't like this.

On top of endless sadness and pain, Emily looks tired. Her hair is tied up in a messy bun and her eyes are red. I assume it's from excessive crying and lack of sleep. I can feel her uneasiness of being in the hospital. She has been here too for almost choking to death after getting too drunk. Her muscles are tight and she crosses her arms, holding her elbows in each hand. She's uncomfortable.

I too hate being here.

I stare at her for a moment, trying to form words that will make sense. She breathes heavily, fighting back her tears. She fails, and eventually they make their way to the corners of her eyes. She places her hand on my chest and kisses my forehead as she releases a sad smile.

I apologize over and over to her even though I know it won't change what happened. I think that deep down she understands, but I know that I have put her in a predicament. Emily needs stability. And at this point, she knows I can't offer that.

She doesn't say much to me. She is still trying to process everything that happened and what she had to do to save me. She is a lot stronger than me. I don't think I would be able to hold it together as much as she has. I don't want her to leave me.

**

Today I am discharging home. I admit, I am feeling better about things with Emily and me. She has been here every day, although I haven't been here long at all. I know she is trying to show me love and comfort and I really couldn't ask for anything more from her.

Emily picks me up and we head to the coffee shop where it all started for us. She places her hand on my thigh, something I often did to her when I was in the driver's seat. I don't mind the silent ride. I don't expect endless conversation right away just like before all of this happened.

As we pull up, my feelings are regenerating as I think about the first real conversation we shared here and how that poor kid wore that ridiculous costume outside. He does not stand there anymore, though. I suppose it's too cold now to stand outside for eight hours doing nothing but waving your hand back and forth and talking to people.

We sit at the same table as before, and it's like all my feelings return from when I first met her. I'm giddy, and nervous about liking a girl as pretty as her. For the hour that we're here, I feel as though she is feeling the same way as I am. I'm making her laugh and she's telling me about her meetings she's been to recently and how she and Amy made up last week.

Amy ended up calling her after going missing for two weeks. No one around town had heard from her, not even her friends from the meeting. Amy ended up going to an inpatient rehab program for a month, and has been much better since moving back home.

As Emily smiles, I see that Amy has brought her some hope back that things can change for the better. I can only pray that she shares this hope for me, too.

*⁣**

I wake up confused at three in the morning with Emily facing me as her eyelids flicker while she is dreaming. Did she move around and wake me up? It couldn't have been her.

Jack invades my dreams unlike he has before. This is the second time he has come. Except, this time, it was more like a nightmare. He's angry with me, like I have done wrong to him. Jack screams as the veins in his neck pop out, spit flying out of his mouth with every word.

"Fucking get it together, Gray!" he repeats as I stand still, unable to say a word. My body stays frozen and I'm afraid to breathe. What have I done to make him act this way?

"I'm sorry," I say to him. "What can I do to make things better?" My voice cracks as my question turns into a nervous breakdown.

"You will lose Emily if you don't."

"Don't what?" I beg, hoping he will give me a more specific answer. But he does not respond. He stares at me for a moment with no facial expression. It's like he's staring through me, looking into nothing. He turns around steadily and leaves me alone.

I have always wondered if dreams of dead people are signs that they are truly trying to get a message through. Or could it be I just coincidentally created that dream in my head from all the shit that has been going on?

The first time I dreamed of Jack he found me hanging out with some of our friends at a pizza place we used to go to that had an arcade attached to it. When I saw him, I thought I was hallucinating, because, although I was so happy to lay eyes on him, I knew that he was dead.

He looked sad and eventually approached me when I moved away from other people. He cried and told me how sorry he was. He didn't have to tell me what for. I already knew. I have a similar feeling now when I tell the same thing to Emily.

Before I could ask Jack where he was, he disappears. Is he still on Earth, or did he make his way to Heaven? I never got closure from that dream. And since then, I have not heard from Jack until tonight.

I look at the clock. Thirty-five minutes have gone by while I sit here trying to make sense of what Jack said to me.

Emily starts to squirm on the bed then stops after placing her arm over my side onto my back like she is hugging me. I think she's the only reason I can fall back asleep.

Emily

I did not break up with Grayson, but I have been spending more time alone than before. The empty space around me has made me feel better.

I often don't pick up his phone calls, and when he texts, I reveal my disinterest through short, one-word answers. At times, I don't even bother to look at my phone.

He's slept over two or three times, but I prefer to fall asleep by myself. There's something about sleeping alone that feels good to me. Maybe it's just that I've been so used to sleeping alone and now having another body lay next to me feels like an invasion of my privacy.

When I first started casting Grayson away from my bed, it felt weird sleeping alone. But after all the years of being the only soul, I quickly adapted back to my natural state.

I'm not intentionally ignoring him, leaving him feeling lonely. I'm just trying to shield myself. I want to keep myself away from all the hurt. Deep down, I think I am preparing myself for this relationship to be severed, and maybe my heart can't endure all the pain at once.

He was discharged from the hospital a little over three weeks ago. Since then, I've made it very obvious to both of us that I haven't been the same. Grayson is having a difficult time opening up to me and letting me know what's on his mind. But so am I.

Our flight is booked for early tomorrow morning. Grayson and I are going to Florida where Grayson's grandmother lives. He hasn't seen her in two or three years, I think. Grayson told me about her when we first met.

When he was younger, she lived right down the road and was very much a big part of his life. It's his mom's mom. She was always a role model for him as a child when Ron would walk in and out of Grayson's life. She was a dependable and trustworthy adult that provided the stability that Ron couldn't.

We planned this trip before everything happened and I think a change of scenery will be good for us. Plus, the weather is still warm down there and it will be nice to relax outside of my tiny apartment.

Tonight, I'll spend the night alone while I try to escape every negative thought that powers through my mind. Although I am trying to make things work, I can already feel that I am deserting his heart. He doesn't know it, but in a way, he has deserted my heart, too.

This feeling in my soul is cold, and unfortunately very familiar to me. Could this be how my mom felt just before she decided she didn't want to claim me anymore?

I could not imagine just abandoning Grayson for the mistakes he's made. Everyone has their issues and I don't think people should be able to determine how poor one's mistakes are.

I look back at one of my notebook entries from a year and a half ago. It's something I wrote after my mom came into the book shop, completely unaware that I had been working there.

I am alone. I am tired.
My mother has left, and has
forced me to fight my battle alone.
I am embarrassed. I am sad.
I am losing faith.

I thought that by writing things on paper, it would snatch the emotions out of my body to a place where they could be locked up in a book for no one to see. But maybe they can't.

I read this entry six more times, and each time, my unpleasant emotions return. It's more than exhausting. The past few weeks have drained me beyond belief regardless of how early I try to fall asleep or how late I sleep in. My body has no idea how to handle the ups and downs. It's like they can change anytime without warning, and when they do, it leaves me more confused.

I make a cup of tea and turn on the television in my room, prepared to doze off any minute now. The lights are dim, giving the room a kiddish feeling as if I'm not allowing all the lights to be fully turned off so I can see the mythical creatures roaming around the room at night.

I'm curled up with fuzzy socks and a space heater next to my bed. A dark loneliness has slowly eaten away at my body. Being alone isn't always the best idea, even when I feel like it is. I wish Grayson were here. I also wish things could be easy with us and I didn't have to feel like a monster by being angry with him.

They say anger is part of the grieving process, and that it's very normal. I know that I don't have to share my feelings with anyone, but I'm ashamed that this is one of the major feelings that has saturated my body since Grayson overdosed.

I suppose I am grieving our relationship.

***

I wake up more excited than I anticipated, knowing that in just a short few hours we will be up in the air heading down to warmth together. For the first time in a while, I can't wait to kiss Grayson. I wish I woke up next to him, but I know I'll have that chance again on our mini vacation.

Although I packed mostly everything the past couple of days, I still need to gather a few more things before leaving my apartment.

Grayson and I have been texting all morning and it's like we're back to where we started in love. I actually feel like answering him today. I don't know how I can feel so terrible one day then feel so optimistic the next.

He's on his way to my house and then we'll leave for the airport. It's still dark outside with no house lights on, presenting like it's the middle of the night. I breathe in the fresh cold air seeping through my window. My apartment is like an icebox that affects my sensitive skin, even with the heat on.

As soon as Grayson gets here, we plan to pack up everything in my car and head to the airport. We're going for almost a week, so we have two large duffle bags and one suitcase filled with our stuff. Grayson is eager to get there. I'm sure he really misses his grandmother.

Airports freak me out. I don't like how crowded and close together everyone must be when going through security. Luckily since our flight is early, the bundled-up group of people is to a minimum. Grayson says if you try and catch a flight in the middle of the day, especially on weekends, it looks like a riot. I thank God we aren't dealing with that right now.

My anxiety rises to its maximum while we sit in our seats awaiting departure with the other planes. It's my first time on a plane. I've heard horror stories on the news of planes going missing without a trace. Months later, scattered broken pieces are discovered at the bottom of the ocean with no survivors to be found. I hope this doesn't scare the shit out of me because I have to do this again in order to get back home.

I look over to Grayson with wide eyes and he begins to laugh at me. It is kind of silly, I suppose. I start laughing too and rest my head on his shoulder as he reaches for my hand to hold it tight.

"This will be fun" he assures me. How the hell is flying with the chance of dying fun to him?

He's crazy, I think to myself as I smile and turn my head to face the window so he doesn't see me. The plane picks up speed and I grip each armrest as if I'm going to fall from the top of a skyscraper. It feels so much faster when you're actually in the plane and not looking from afar.

My stomach drops as we lift into the air, reminding me of the first time Grayson kissed me. Suddenly, I feel like a young teenager high on love. I understand now why he thinks flying is fun. It's almost like we are on a carnival ride together.

He can see the relief on my face, and I admit to him that I was way too scared for no good reason. It was not nearly as terrifying as I had imagined. He puts his arm around me and looks into my eyes with his face almost touching mine as he speaks softly into my ear.

"You trusted me."

Jack

Once they land in Florida together, it's as if they left all their sorrows back home. Their Florida vacation is a new and exciting escape for them. I watch as they hold hands, leaving the terminal to retrieve their luggage.

As they wait for the belt to circle around with their suitcase, Grayson nudges Emily's shoulder. They stand in silence, with happiness painted all over their faces. If I didn't know any better, I would have thought they had known each other their whole lives.

They run to catch a cab while looking at each other and grinning. This is the first time I've seen true happiness between them since Grayson almost died. That day was a tough pill for both of them to swallow, but I think they are finally crawling out of that dark time together.

They ride to the resort they're staying at, which is almost on the ocean. The resort's beachfront view was hypnotizing, and Grayson could not resist the scenery despite the cost. It was a surprise for Emily.

Grayson debated staying at his grandmother's, but he wanted a more private place to be with Emily in an attempt to rekindle their relationship together. He was able to book this resort last minute.

As they enter their condo, Emily rushes to the balcony, placing her hands on the railing while throwing her head back. She begins to sob.

"What's wrong, Baby?" Grayson asks her in a panic, afraid she is upset with him again. She opens her mouth and pauses for a moment, looking back at him as tears continue to stream down her face. She shares something with Grayson that he had not expected her to say.

"I've never seen the ocean."

He's shocked at her response, but grateful that her tears are filled with happiness and exhilaration—something Grayson has not seen in her for quite some time.

They decide to spend their day exploring the resort and beach before going to Grayson's grandmother's for dinner.

There is a pool filled with a sand bottom, giving their feet the feeling of touching down on the ocean bottom. It's located in the center of the resort, surrounded by all the condos. The trees sway in the warm air and music plays everywhere they walk.

They haven't stopped laughing and smiling since they landed and I worry that when Grayson finds out the news, it will ruin the entire trip—the last hope of him trying to win Emily back for good. This is his chance to show her that she is the only thing he needs, and he will sacrifice whatever is necessary for her to know that. If he suffers any more loss, I fear he may turn the wrong way to cope.

They lay out by the pool and jacuzzi for several hours without being interrupted by any company. Grayson talks nonstop as Emily lays there and listens. She ends up falling asleep in her chair, exhausted from waking up early and traveling. I laugh while Grayson continues to talk— he doesn't know what is going on behind her sunglasses.

Grayson pauses as his phone rings. It's his grandmother wondering what time Emily and he will be going over for dinner. He tells her around seven or so, and then his grandmother provides some small talk without any expression in her voice. Grayson finds it very odd, but assumes her old age is getting to her. As he attempts to wrap up the conversation, she says nothing besides, "I love you," in a very serious tone.

Grayson is so mesmerized as he stares at Emily's sleeping body that he thinks nothing of it. Except, I know why she has said it that way. And soon, Grayson will know too.

Emily

By the time I wake up, I can tell it's too late to attempt more sun block. My skin burns with heat, leaving my body feeling warmer than my liking.

My body is dark pink and the skin on my chest begins to peel upwards. As my eyes travel down my body, I haven't seen the worst yet— my feet. They boil with red lumps that will eventually turn into blisters. When I move my arms away from my body, I can feel a soreness at the crevices of my armpits. It's not the ideal way to start of a vacation, but things could be a lot worse.

I'm a bit nervous to meet Grayson's grandmother because I'm worried she will not like me. Even though Grayson's mom loves me, my own mom does not. So, I find my anxiety to be expected. I have a hard time pleasing certain people. I suppose it all depends on the person, whether they are the understanding type or the ignorant asshole type.

Grayson and I walk back up toward our condo as I wince every time my feet touch the ground. I jokingly ask Grayson to carry me and before I can move further, he scoops me up onto his back for a piggyback ride. My feet are thankful.

Small, lizard-like animals scurry across the stone walkway leading toward the door to get back inside. I don't think I could ever get used to these creepy-crawlers even if I lived here. They are everywhere, emerging from hiding spaces I'd least expect.

During our travels and our time here, I haven't even thought to wonder whether Grayson is using. He's been clean since leaving the hospital and maybe it's foolish of me to think he's completely done with drugs. But I don't know. I guess an addict is never truly done with drugs because the thought will always linger and it constantly nudges at the brain, attempting to make its toxicity known again.

At the same time, I feel as though it would be unhealthy for me to not worry about him. If I didn't care, this love would eventually eat me alive and kill us both. Because I know how easy it is to be well and then fall back down to rock bottom. It only takes one single choice.

I have had an outfit planned for this night since before I even started packing. I've chosen a light-yellow sun dress. Something cute, yet comfortable. I want to make a good first impression.

I don't wear too much makeup. I don't want to scare her away. We take our rental car to her house which is about twenty miles east of where we're staying. The clouds gather together and the sun hides, opposite of how the weather has been all day.

We pull up to her to house which looks like it was built from 1800's, yet it stands out like a modern-day castle that anyone would be lucky to live in.

Her driveway is gated and for a second I wonder if this is the right place. Grayson has never been here before so he really wouldn't know either. We have the right address though, and his grandmother did say we would need a code to get through.

As we drive up the brick driveway, green grass surrounds us and squirrels lurk beyond the oak trees.

The house is dark inside, despite the daylight's attempt to squeeze its way through the cracks of the blinds. The furniture is coated with a thin layer of a plastic cover. It's quiet. The only movement is the dust in the air as we walk through the hallways trying to figure out where his grandmother is. It does not look like anyone lives here.

She comes out of the bathroom and is surprised that we have already entered her home. She must have lost track of time.

"Hi, boy!" she screams to Grayson as she throws her arms forward inviting him in for a long, tight hug. She holds him with a secure grip, as if he's a precious newborn baby that's more delicate than glass. Her face slowly turns red and I wonder if she's about to burst into tears from being so happy.

He pulls away from her and turns to me as he places his arm on my back, tugging me closer to his body.

In a serious yet cheerful voice he introduces me as if he is so proud to call me his.

"This is my girlfriend, Emily."

She responds quicker than I imagined she would as she thrusts her body toward mine to give me one of those big grandmotherly hugs.

"I have heard so many great things about you! Welcome to our family!"

Woah. Overly inviting is my initial thought, although I do like the sound of her saying *our family.* Grayson must have put in some pretty solid words for her to invite me in like that when it's our first-time meeting and I've barely said two words to her.

She invites us to follow her to the kitchen where she is preparing dinner. Turkey and homemade gravy fill the air in the hallway leading out to the living room and kitchen open floor plan. This house is so elegant, and I question how such a cute old lady can maintain such an enormous house.

She instructs us to sit down as she finishes up and prepares the plates to serve us. We sit at a large rectangle table, with Grayson on my left. He places his hand on my knee and gives me a smile sensing that I am somewhat uncomfortable and still nervous to be meeting his grandmother, who is practically a second mom to him.

She sets up placemats and brings the plates to the table before sitting across from Grayson and me. We all begin to dig into our food at the same time. Home cooked — a meal people can hardly get sick of.

As we're finishing up, she takes a large sip of ice water and starts talking about moving again.

"What would you think about Grammy moving back up near you guys?"

"I mean, that would be awesome," Grayson says, but I can tell by the tone of his voice that he is confused as to why she would consider that idea. She loves it here in Florida. She has a beautiful house and doesn't have to worry about shoveling snow out of her driveway in the winter.

She begins to speak again as she takes her fork and pushes around the remaining food on her plate.

"You know, when your mother first told me about being sick, I was worried about not being around for you guys. But then I thought, why don't I just move back up there to be close to the both of you."

Sick? My stomach drops into my lap as I look over at Grayson, wondering if he has any idea what she's talking about. He has never mentioned to me that his mom was sick. I can see his face mirrors mine—a face of pure confusion and shock.

"Mom is sick?" he says to her. His voice cracks and his eyes widen as he impatiently waits for her to explain this to him.

His grandmother slowly frowns, and she lets her head fall to her chest, realizing Grayson had no idea. She looks upset, knowing that she is the wrong person to tell him. It should be his mom.

"Oh dear," she begins again. She looks as though she has no idea how to handle this situation she has put him in.

"Your mother has pancreatic cancer, I'm afraid...a kind that is tough to cure."

Her voice trails off and I imagine her trying not to think about losing her own daughter.

We sit in silence for what feels like an eternity. I'm afraid to move. I stay still like a statue as I let Grayson try and process this the way he needs to.

Instead of responding, he stands up and walks out of the room. The silence continues as his grandmother and I stare at each other for a moment. She grimaces as she attempts to hold her tears in. Her bottom lip quivers and she tucks it under her top lip to try and make it stop. She looks in the direction where Grayson has broken free from this wretched conversation.

She stands up after deciding to go after him, but I stop her immediately, knowing that she will make him feel worse in this moment.

"He needs a minute." I tell her. She smiles at me, grateful that Grayson has a person like me that knows him so well. Surely, she does not want to exacerbate this situation.

After a couple of minutes, Grayson returns to the table with his head tilted downward, not looking at either of us. He clears his throat, so he can form words without sounding as if he's completely broken down.

"She didn't tell me."

His grandmother has no idea what to say to him. I can tell by the look in her eyes that she wants to console him but has no idea how. A tint of guilt is embedded in her lips, and she shivers feeling the sadness of Grayson's face.

He looks at me and makes eye contact for the first time since leaving the table.

"I think I want to go home." Again, he leaves the table, heading toward the front door where he doesn't hesitate to leave the house without looking back.

I can't believe this is happening. An exciting trip to see a long-distance family member has now turned into probably the worst day of his life.

Grayson

How could she not tell me? Her own son deserves to know if she's dying or not. I know she didn't plan for me to find out this way, but why did she feel like she couldn't tell me herself? Questions are flooding my head and I want to scream.

I can't believe that all this time I didn't know. I wonder how long my mom has known. Has she thought about telling me? Was she going to wait until she was actively dying to mention it to me? I'm pissed off.

I think it's selfish of her not to tell me and maybe that makes me a fucked-up person, but I don't care. Except for Emily, she is really all that I have left at home. Grandma is a whole plane ride away. She knows this. So, what tempted her to keep this vital secret from me?

My mom and I have been through a lot together, and we have always been there for each other to go to whenever we need to talk. Except, her feelings must have changed. She cannot look me in the eyes and tell me she may very well die soon. Just selfish.

I get in the car and wait for Emily to follow me out. I'm sure she's feeling just as uncomfortable as I am. I have left her in a large house with a vulnerable elderly woman who she just met a couple hours earlier.

A few minutes go by and I see her walking out the front door turning back to wave my grandmother goodbye. She sits in the passenger seat and says nothing. We sit there for a minute and without turning toward me, she tries to find words to make me feel better.

"I'm just...so sorry Grayson." I start the car to leave this miserable house. Part of me feels bad for just leaving my grandmother. I mean, she didn't do anything wrong. She didn't know that I didn't know. In a way, I'm glad she said something because I may not have known the truth until one morning when my mom doesn't wake up and I find her in her bed just like Emily found me. It's just terrible to think about.

I drive us to the beach, where I hope the sound of the crashing waves will soothe my brain and my broken heart. I know Emily will like this too. She'd never seen the ocean up until yesterday, never mind touched the water with her bare skin.

She holds my hand and smiles when she figures out where I'm taking us. We park and sit in the car while listening to waves and a group of people in front of us laughing around a campfire.

I look toward her as I can feel her excited grip on my hand. "Are you ready for this?"

She squeezes my hand and then darts out of the door like she's in a life or death situation and needs to escape as quickly as possible.

Together, we hold hands as she's practically dragging me across the warm sand toward the water. I've never seen such white sand. Pictures my grandmother has shown me just don't do it justice.

We arrive at the line where the ocean meets dry sand and wait there for the wave to ripple back toward our toes. The water has a clear green shade to it, light enough to be able to see straight to the bottom where the rocks and critters live.

She closes her eyes and breathes in the fresh salty air. Emily moves her arms outward as if she's flying. The warm water fills up around her feet and she squeals like the water is cold. She begins to laugh and gestures to me that we should go in deeper even though we are fully clothed.

For those few minutes, I forget that I am sad. That's what Emily does to me. She makes me feel happy even when I feel like breaking down.

My smile slowly turns into a frown as I look out to the open water where the sun is now hiding. She pulls me back onto the beach, silently telling me it's okay for us to leave.

I fall to my knees as I hold my hands to my face as uncontrollable tears leak down my cheeks. I think I just need to go home.

Emily

He falls asleep as soon as his head hits the pillow. He sleeps soundly in his day clothes and unbrushed teeth. Sleep is his best option right now. I'm glad it was this easy for him to fall asleep. I'm exhausted and have been worried that I'll stay up all night trying to console him even though there's nothing I can say or do to make things better for him.

As I get ready for bed, I wonder to myself if Grayson has said anything to his mom. Has he told her everything is going fine here? Or has he let her know that he's aware of her terrible secret?

I wonder what it's been like for her. She's so used to taking care of Grayson. Has she forgotten to take care of herself? Maybe she's been waiting for the right time to tell Grayson although I'm not too sure if there's ever a right time to tell someone you'll be dead within six months. His grandmother told me the prognosis right before I left her house to follow Grayson. It made everything worse. I don't know how much more loss he can take.

I cuddle up behind him and place my arm down his thigh. I breathe in his scent on the back of his neck. He feels like home. I hold him tight, as if I'm able to shield him from all distress and misfortune. I wish that my arms were powerful enough to make him not hurt so much.

***

The sun is shining through the naked window, yet he doesn't wake. He's been laying in the same position on the bed for six hours now. I've seen him get up once early in the morning to use the bathroom, but nothing since.

He's placed his head under the pillow as the rest of his body is submerged in cotton blankets. He has one arm that he occasionally sticks out for fresh air, but that is the only movement I've seen since early this morning.

I cannot begin to imagine how he is feeling. The one person in his life who has accepted him fully even during his dark times, will die before we know it.

I talk to him, but he does not answer me. Although he's probably sleeping a lot, I know he has heard me. He rubs his thumb and pointer finger together when I call his name, a little sign he shows me that he isn't completely ignoring me, but enough to tell me he doesn't want to talk. I don't push for conversation because he is the type of person who copes in silence and I have to respect that.

We are supposed to be here for three more days, although I don't see him wanting to do much more than bury himself in bed. I wonder if he wants to leave early, but I decide not to ask quite yet. Maybe he will figure things out in his mind and let me know what he wants to do when he's ready.

I walk down to the beach, where day life is a lot different than nightlife. A group of people are playing volleyball with a net that is set up in the sand. They yell to each other as the teammates high five with each point they get.

Across from them, is a young couple with two children who are maybe three or four-years-old. They build sandcastles together as the parents prepare lunch under their five-foot tent.

I sit down on the hot sand, the tiny grains of heat burning the back of my thighs. I wish I could sit here and never move. In just a short few days, I will be back in the cold weather, resuming a hopeful life with Grayson.

I know that things will be screwed up when we get back, though. Grayson has found out the worst news of his life and can't stand the thought of losing another close person to Heaven.

Jack

They cut their trip short and head for the airport. Once again, they travel through a non-crowded airport where it's past dinner time and most people have come and gone for the day. It's quiet. People are tired of traveling, including Grayson.

His eyelids hang low and he drags his feet as if there are ten-pound weights attached to his ankles. Still, I don't think he's brushed his teeth.

Grayson sleeps sideways on two chairs as they wait to be called for boarding the plane.

He has not eaten since dinner at his grandmother's...the day he found out.

Emily sits quietly, reading a book while offering her lap as a pillow so he can sleep. That is, after all, the only thing he's been well capable of doing since that evening.

Emily's attention shifts to Grayson's soundless body. She stares at his face, wishing she could take away all the pain he's had to endure in his lifetime.

Maybe Grayson's dad, Ron, will come back to him. Maybe he's straightened out and we just don't know it. Or maybe, he will never come back.

He is predictably unpredictable. A dangerous quality to make of a decent father. He's simply not capable of being one.

I don't believe that Grayson or his mom have had contact with him, so he must not know of her condition. Not that he'd care much. But I would hope he would make an attempt, something he's never been able to do since Grayson was born.

Emily must wonder if his mom has been seeking treatment and just not telling them. Or has her fatal diagnosis wiped away any hope of trying to get better? Leaving her with one option. Death.

I hate how I know the answer to that but I'm not able to communicate it with them. Maybe if they knew, they could live these last few hours down south with some ease, without feeling left out in the dark.

God has a plan. He has a plan for Grayson, and he has one for his mom, too. If only I could talk to Grayson, it would make things better for him. He needs me right now.

As the attendant calls for boarding, Grayson sluggishly sits up and looks around as though he has forgotten where he was.

"It's time for us to go," Emily says quietly.

They stand together, gathering their belongings. Grayson walks slowly to the end of the line of doom leading back to his sick mom. He's obviously not happy to go home, but he knows that he needs to go.

It's one of the better choices he's made since being clean. His outlook on life is different now, yet the addict in Grayson is still there.

The trip home is nothing but a long ride of agony that will be topped off with more fear as soon as they step foot onto land. It's just another step closer. The moment of being home is approaching faster than he thinks, and I don't think he's ready for it. For her.

His mom has lost a substantial amount of weight in the last two weeks because her cancer has progressed quicker than anyone could have expected. Even her doctors.

Her ribs are beginning to peak through her thin, pale skin. The clothes she wears are baggy, an attempt she makes to hide her bones sticking through her regular clothes. Her bones are brittle, making even a tiny fall a catastrophic injury for her.

She wears a beanie hat that covers her hair that's been slowly thinning, not from treatment, but rather from possible genetics and not getting the proper nutrition. It's traumatizing for her to watch the once beautiful surface of her soul evaporate before her eyes.

Grayson and Emily have landed safely.

"I have to go to the bathroom, hold on a sec," he tells her. She waits outside for him, clasping her hands together as her nerves grow the closer they get to home. Her stomach aches constantly, as she worries how Grayson will react once home.

Grayson sits on the toilet with his torso bent forward as he puts his palms to his face, covering his eyes. He sits in silence as an abundance of tears pour from his eyes. His silence soon breaks as he starts a hysterical panic of hyperventilating.

His voice roars into a loud cry as he has completely lost control of his emotions. It grows louder, and his face is bright red, as though he is not taking in enough oxygen. He bangs his hands on the stall door as he screams.

Without hesitation, Emily races into the men's bathroom, not giving a shit about who else is in there. This is why I love her.

She bursts through the stall door where Grayson sits huddled into a ball. She holds his body to her core, and tears up, pressing her face to the top of his head.

They hold each other in the stall, crying together, while wishing people didn't have to fucking die so much.

***

The cold breeze of winter hits their skin as they step out to the sidewalk where traffic sits and the sound of beeping horns echo under the airport ceiling.

They take a bus back into town, where they have an Uber meeting them to drive them back to Grayson's mom's house. Grayson hasn't shown much emotion since the incident in the bathroom. He sits next to the window and stares out at the naked trees as they make their way toward home.

Grayson will not handle being at home well. I know it. As they near, his thoughts consume him and he's not thinking logically. He is truly a ticking time bomb, awaiting a massive explosion of emotions.

As they pull into the driveway, Emily begins to gather her things, but Grayson sits there without movement. The Uber driver is confused.

"Sir?" he says, looking in the rearview mirror back at Grayson.

"Oh." His voice trails off. "Right. Thanks for the ride."

He's afraid to walk through the front door. He stands in the cold waiting at the door as if he is unsure whether he should walk in. He inches forward, then stops and waits a minute before taking another step.

"Take your time," Emily says, assuring him it's okay to be feeling the way he does.

Emily places her hand in Grayson's, nodding her head to him that it's time to walk inside. He squeezes her hand and reaches his other hand to open the door.

"Hey Baby," his mom says with the biggest smile I've ever seen on her face. Part of her smile is hiding some of the guilt she bears from not telling Grayson sooner, and for Grayson finding out on vacation from someone other than herself.

Grayson sits beside her, studying her features that have drastically changed. I think Grayson will always remember her as the beautiful woman he got to call mom. She was truly stunning.

He doesn't speak, but she knows he's happy to be home with her. Together, they lay on the couch cuddled up, and fall asleep together within minutes.

Emily sits on the recliner where she watches them. It's in this moment when Emily realizes how much this will break Grayson. He clings to her like a baby koala clings to its mother—attached no matter the movement or situation—hanging on for dear life.

Emily knows what happens when he breaks. What he seeks out to feel better.

As her thoughts consume her, her eyes begin to close and she falls into a much-needed deep sleep. She dreams of good dreams and sleeps through the ruckus that Grayson causes.

***

It's the afternoon now, and Emily awakens panicked when she looks at the clock and doesn't see Grayson on the couch anymore.

"Where is he?" she asks louder than she means to and apologizes to Grayson's mom right after her words come out, not giving her time to answer the question right away.

"He got upset," she says looking down to the floor. "So, he left."

"Left to go where?" Emily asks, anger growing in her voice and she is unable to control her volume now.

"I don't know dear, but he'll be back. I know he will."

Emily gets up in a hurry and grabs her coat to run for the front door, nearly tripping over her own feet.

"Stop." His mom commands. Emily looks back at her with her forehead wrinkled upward, confused. "Give him some time."

Emily nods her head, and walks back to the recliner, realizing that this situation is all too familiar. Just a few days prior, she was the one giving his grandmother the same advice when she tried to run after Grayson.

Emily knows that time is what Grayson needs, so she will grant him that. His mom invites her to hang around the house until he's back.

Something that doesn't happen quite as soon as they expected.

Emily

He has been missing for twenty-four hours. His mom says he's fine, that he's just gone to deal with his emotions. I suppose her declining health has impacted her judgment of her son.

If he was fine, he'd be here with me. Not somewhere off the grid without notifying a soul. I don't say this because I don't think he's okay, I say this because *I know* he's not okay. I fear danger may cross paths with him. The kind of danger he puts on himself.

He should be here with his mom. His dying mom.

Grayson's phone has either died or been turned off, not allowing me to track him even with assistance from the phone company. *Just fucking useless,* I say to myself as the operator directs me to get help from the police.

Don't they understand that's the first thing I would do after looking and not finding him? The police haven't said any shit to me that's been helpful. Since Grayson is a legal adult, he is free to go wherever he wants. Unless they have reason to believe something bad happened to him, they can't do much.

The second officer I spoke to asked me where I thought he would go. "Is there someplace he really likes to be...somewhere he feels comfortable?" He carelessly inquires, digging for an answer so he can be done with me and carry on with his day.

"No," my voice becoming defensive, "he's literally always with me. And now he's not." My voice trails off as I realize I'm not going to get the immediate help I need to find him. Just another useless person.

I look everywhere. No one has seen him. No one has heard from him. He's vanished into thin air without leaving a trace of evidence pointing to where he might go.

Goddammit, Grayson, I murmur to myself. "I won't stop looking for you," I say aloud as though he is able to hear me from wherever he may be.

***

He's now been gone for thirty hours and I fear his demons will come back to haunt him. He's vulnerable and alone. *Please God, don't let him do this again.*

His mom is a mess. And not really because he's gone, but because she's slowly dying. She has a hospice nurse that comes to the house daily. There's dust on the tables and dirt on the floor. She is unable to clean. She is unable to do a lot of normal things. Brushing her teeth has become a monumental task, causing extreme fatigue.

She sleeps a lot, but when she is awake, she's resting on the couch, hardly ever moving except to use the bathroom.

I've been staying at her house to help her out with things since Grayson has left.

"He'll be back," she reassures me.

It isn't the coming back that I'm deeply afraid of. It's *how* he is when he comes back. High or not high.

I finish making us breakfast, although I'm not in any emotional state to eat a full meal. It makes me sick to my stomach just looking the full plate of food that I've prepared.

I think about inspecting Grayson's room in search of a clue that will lead me to where he is. I'm fearful to enter the room that has scarred the core of my soul. The last entrance left me hysterical while I watched Grayson overdose.

I stare at his door. I know he's not behind it, but something makes my hand hesitates to touch the doorknob. What am I afraid of now?

The last time I needed to go through this door, I had thrust it open without any hesitation. I practically threw my body into it, ready to run right through it, breaking it into tiny pieces.

I try and convince myself that the feeling of entering will not be the same as last time. Scratch that. I know it won't be the same. But the edge of anxiety doesn't go away because I know Grayson isn't in there. I don't know where he is, or if he's okay.

And that makes me sad.

I finally gather the courage to make a move. I open the door about five inches and place my head in the small crack to peek through without fully entering. His room is clean. Much cleaner than he's ever left it.

I step through the doorway where I stand adjacent to his bed. It's made neatly, and his floor is bare. I can still see the marks from the vacuum cleaner.

His tables and television, unlike downstairs, carry no dust. All of his clothes are folded or hung up. It doesn't appear that he's taken any with him.

I sit on his floor for a moment, hugging myself as I begin to shake. I don't think I've ever been this worried about someone in my entire life.

I tilt my head down to rest it on my knees as tears stream down my face. A brown silhouette sits before me. I blink hard to unload the water that has built up in my eyes, causing my blurred vision.

I stare at his desk. It is too neat. Grayson was never really organized. His pens stand in a holder, while all his other notebooks and papers are stacked in a pile to the far left. Except, there's one thing there that's out in the open. A piece of paper.

I walk closer, questioning why this paper has been placed like this, neatly placed smack dab in the middle. It's half a piece of notebook paper with only a few words written on it.

My heart races as I start to read the evidence Grayson has left behind for me, although it's not formally addressed to me.

I'll be back. Don't come looking for me.

I'm sorry.

He is gone.

And he doesn't want me to find him.

Jack

She continues her slow, miserable slope of declination. The hours she's spent without Grayson next to her have left her lonely mind deprived of her son. A feeling no mother should ever have to endure.

As the grandfather clock standing across from where she lays moves hour to hour, she begins losing hope that Grayson will indeed come home.

She gets closer to death as the hours pass, but then again, aren't we all dying? I think that we all start to die as soon as were born. When we enter the world, we're only entering a timeline toward death.

She doesn't know if what she's doing is right for Grayson. Or what she isn't doing. She watches as Emily fights to find something, in pure fright that she may not find anything at all—or him.

She wishes she wasn't so weak. Everything is so exhausting. Breathing is exhausting.

Maybe Emily was right. Something is off. Maybe they should be doing more to find him.

She's finally able to fall asleep after Emily has left the house. I take advantage of this time to pay her a visit.

She sits at the park near the house she grew up in. It must really mean something to her. She doesn't look sick anymore. Her skin is so vibrant, and her hair is long and neatly pulled back into a ponytail.

She sits on a bench with her legs crossed as she scribbles in her notebook. As I get close, I walk toward her with caution, fearing she will be alarmed at seeing her son's dead friend. She hasn't seen me since right before I was buried.

I walk up a few stairs and stay on the stone path that leads to her bench. A large gust of wind blows her notebook pages. She looks up to where I stand, far enough away to keep her from touching me, but close enough that she can hear me.

"Jack? Oh my…is this really you? But you…"

"Hi. Yes. How are you doing?"

"Am I dead?" she starts looking around as though she has lost touch of where she is all of a sudden.

"Where are we?"

I don't tell her where we are, or explain why we are here. Instead, I want to make sure I can make her comfortable so we can talk.

"It's okay…you're not dead. I just wanted to talk to you. It's been a long time, huh?" I offer a soft smile and she pats the wood beside her, inviting me to sit down.

She's no longer scared to die. It's not all that scary, really. I explain to her how I've been watching everything. She giggles with relief and takes a deep breath. She's shocked this conversation is really happening right now.

I tell her it's okay to let go. She can't stay when she's supposed to be in Heaven. It's a hard thing to do, but I tell her how I know Grayson will be as okay as he can be.

He will learn to let go too, and live his life with Emily in a way he's learned because of her.

I will be waiting for her.

She has another angel up here too waiting for her—one that she's never met.

Grayson

I'm not trying to make everyone freak out. I just need time alone. Time to think. Time to cry. I need to do this without being bothered. So, I shut my phone off and disappear.

I'm thinking about drugs. I want to do them. I know exactly where to go to get them. I plan to do them, but something is making me hesitate to leave this pitched tent I've set up in the middle of the woods.

Maybe I'm too cold to move. I shiver so hard that my muscles are becoming sore. Maybe this is God telling me I'm finally free and it's time to go home to my dying mother. Or maybe, I just need to suck it up and go get my drugs.

I'm not running away. I just want time to be undistracted from what I need to do, and a place to do it.

I read online once that if you put cooking spray on a tent, it will cause the snow to slide off instead of piling up on it. So, I've brought that just in case the weather turns on me.

It must be near freezing. My entire body is masked with goosebumps, and I only brought one blanket, which is my mom's. I only wear the clothes on my back, which I've been in for quite some time now.

I sit in my tent curled up, waiting for something to happen. Am I stupid for thinking this is the way to go about things? Just cast myself into the woods and hope things will get better for me.

Things won't get better because this doesn't change the fact that my mom is withering away in our living room. I'm not ready for her to leave me. And I'm sure she's not ready to leave me either.

I can remember the first time my mother left me to go to school. It was pre-school now that I think about it. I suppose I acted as any other young child would—scared and in constant withdrawal of my caretaker whenever she wasn't with me.

The entire day I cried and hid under the raised sandbox they had inside. How terrible. This is my first memory of being alive, and even at twenty-five, I remember it so well.

Soon I would learn that my mom wasn't gone forever, and in fact, she would be coming back to get me by the end of each day. Even as an adult, the thought of her never coming back for me scares the absolute shit out of me.

I know this time, she won't be coming back, yet I keep a tiny grain of hope close to my heart that resonates in me.

***

My old dealer hides out in the same spot and I'm going to find him. I walk through the woods, the hard ground pushing back at my feet with every step.

The trees are bare, so I stay deep away from the road so no one can see me. I will walk the woods as long as I can before I have to make a turn on the road.

Snowflakes begin to fall from the sky. The first snow of the year. I stand and look up as

I close my eyes and put my hands out to catch them. Jack and I loved playing in the snow as kids.

As I approach the road, I look both ways to make sure no cars are coming, but more importantly, that there isn't a soul around that will lay eyes on me. I walk briskly across the street where a trail starts which will take me behind an abandoned gas station. That's where my guy hangs around.

The trail is narrower than I remember. Dead branches coat the solid ground that's beginning to have a thin layer of snow. I walk quickly as the wind gradually picks up, blowing directly into my face.

My cheeks are numb, and my nose is raining drops of warm fluid, but I have nothing to wipe with. Just when I think I can't get any colder, the snow picks up.

Large snowflakes fall at a rapid speed, covering my body completely. I am not fast enough to control the amount of snow on me because flakes continue to stick to my coat after every swipe I make down my arm. Jack's memory crowds my mind, and I stop in my tracks.

Is this him? The snow, I mean. Is he telling me to go home? I'm at the end of the trail and I can see my old dealer standing under a pine tree smoking a cigarette while he scrolls on his phone.

He must be meeting someone, and I have come just at the right time. Before I step out of the woods, a cold rush of pain fills my chest cavity.

It's a familiar feeling, one that comes when I know I'm doing something wrong. I fight the pain that has now moved into a pulsating throb in my stomach. I know I shouldn't be here.

I've come a long way since I've been with Emily. And even since Jack has died. I'm sure he never thought I would get to where I am. Hell, I didn't think I would either.

I gaze up at the trees, which have now collected the glowing white snow. It's so pretty.

At this moment, I wish I was with Emily.

She's my home.

I don't know what the fuck I'm doing.

Emily

Grayson's mom has been eating snacks throughout the day, but hardly anything nutritional. She eats a cracker here and a pretzel there. I make mint tea for the both of us. It's her favorite. It's the one thing I know I can get into her stomach.

We sit together and talk—that's really the only we can do other than sit in silence, panicking over whether Grayson is dead or not. *Okay*, or not.

I learn that she was adopted right away after she was born. Her birth mother was only fourteen years old, hardly a teenager. It was an easy decision to put her up for adoption, with little insight on her own life itself, never mind another tiny human's.

They never crossed paths after that day.

She was adopted by two loving, dedicated parents who couldn't have children of their own.

"I couldn't imagine growing up with anyone else besides them," she tells me.

I never knew this before. And I don't know if Grayson knows it either.

As she got older, she became more curious about her birth mother—a curiosity she was ashamed to mention because she didn't want her parents to be offended that she sought more truth to her life.

Still, she didn't learn much. After some heavy research and help from one of her high school best friends, they learned that her mother was murdered at the age of twenty-seven in Los Angeles.

She stopped being curious after that.

And never told her parents what she learned.

***

Grayson opens the back-sliding door unannounced and sits at the old wooden kitchen table. His hands sit on his lap and he tucks his legs under his seat. He looks content—his face muscles soft, he does not carry anger for his mom as he had before.

Something has changed.

His eyes lock with mine and he doesn't blink. He opens his mouth and then closes it, waiting for me to say something first. There's nothing he can say at this moment for me to dismiss my anger toward him.

My heart races with bittersweet love because, although I am so happy to see him in front of my eyes, I'm pissed off.

"Where the fuck were you?" I scream at Grayson as I throw my hands through the air and walk briskly toward him. He flinches backward and I'm sure he thinks I'm going to slap him.

"I told you he would come back," his mom says, glaring at me. Woah. Why is she bitching at me? Her cancer is making her loopy. She's been saying inappropriate shit at all the wrong times without even realizing how out of line she is. Especially to the hospice nurse, who's only trying to help her.

She warns me not to yell at him. I grab his arm and drag him down the hallway into one of the guest bedrooms, slamming the door shut to make a point of how angry I am.

I look at him with sad eyes like I'm giving him a *how could you do this to me* kind of look.

"I thought you were dead or something." I begin to cry, and he holds me tight, apologizing that he left a without telling anyone where he was going.

"I just needed some time away," he explains. I can't help but interrogate him.

"Away from what? Your mother who could die any day now? How could you just leave her? She was barely concerned you were gone. She's fucking losing it."

He looks at me with disappointment, lips frowning down to his chin. A look I haven't seen before. I'm trying to read it.

"Grayson," I say as my voice goes down an octave by the time I get to the end of his name.

"Did you?"

"Did I do what?"

"Did you use?" I press him with a sarcastic tone, because he knows what I'm asking but still made me say it.

"No... Emily, I swear. I—I was going too. But I didn't. I swear it to you."

Relief.

He stutters as words keep falling from his mouth, "I didn't do it!"

He didn't.

His voice isn't defensive, but rather honest, with a smear of hope, begging me to believe him.

And I do.

We stand in the middle of the room holding each other like we have never done before. It's a remarkable milestone for Grayson. He did not let his temptations win this time.

This time, Grayson wins.

Two Short Months Later

Grayson

She died on a Sunday.

The Lord's day.

It's a day I wish to one day forget, but for now, it will sleep next to me at night.

Emily and I walked downstairs where the hospice nurse alerted us before we could take our last step.

"She just passed, very peaceful and painless. I'm so very sorry for your loss."

This wasn't the first time I'd seen a dead body. Another person. Gone. Out of my life.

She pre-arranged her services, knowing I would not be able to emotionally handle doing that on my own, even with Emily's help. It's just not something a kid in his twenties ever thinks he'll have to do.

She was laid to rest on a Wednesday—all our family, friends, even neighbors, were in attendance. One man stood in the far back of the crowd of people under a small tree, his face shaded between a mix of branches and overcast.

He walked closer as we prayed in unison, his lips moving with every word spoken. It was Ron. I never knew Ron knew how to pray.

The shock that charged my body was one I had never felt before while laying eyes on the man I was supposed to call Dad. It was the first time in my life I had been happy to see him.

I learned that he had moved back to town after finding out about mom's sickness. He told me no matter how many times he left us, he loved us more than we could understand. He always thought about us. He knew he would never be good enough for my mom, who was nothing short of a saint in my eyes.

We rebuilt our relationship entirely. I knew my mom would be so happy for that.

That day brought us back together and it stayed that way for days to come. He never left me again.

***

It's crazy isn't it? How the most terrible things in the world bring people together? I never knew hurt could create such bright and beautiful things, my heart could almost heal from all the bad.

I'm happy. Even with everything that's happened to me, I know I'm supposed to be happy. It's what Jack would want. It's what my mom would want.

I get to be happy with the most amazing woman by my side.

Finally, I am right where I'm supposed to be.

Made in the USA
Coppell, TX
12 October 2022